GAACONOMICS
The Secret Life of Money in the GAA

GAAconomics

The Secret Life of Money in the GAA

MICHAEL MOYNIHAN

Gill & Macmillan

Gill & Macmillan
Hume Avenue, Park West, Dublin 12
with associated companies throughout the world
www.gillmacmillanbooks.ie

© Michael Moynihan 2013
978 07171 5453 1

Index compiled by Kate Murphy
Typography design by Make Communication
Print origination by Síofra Murphy
Printed and bound by ScandBook AB, Sweden

This book is typeset in Minion 12.5/15.5 pt.

The paper used in this book comes from the wood pulp
of managed forests. For every tree felled, at least one
tree is planted, thereby renewing natural resources.

A CIP catalogue record for this book is available from
the British Library.

5 4 3 2 1

For Marjorie, Clara and Bridget

CONTENTS

ACKNOWLEDGMENTS

Thanks first and foremost to Fergal Tobin of Gill & Macmillan for backing this project at a time when all sports books seem to be celebrity biographies. He didn't even get mad when I missed a deadline, which is a dangerous precedent.

Thanks also to the many people who were patient enough to let me stumble to the end of never-ending questions which often drifted miles away from the point—and provide cogent, interesting answers in response. Everyone I spoke to was helpful—sometimes too helpful, suggesting other people to speak to, which meant extra work but which ultimately benefited the book.

A particular thank you to John Considine for helping at the start, when I was flailing around trying to get some idea where to go and who to approach. He helped his club Sars win the Cork County along the way: a man of many talents.

My gratitude also to my colleagues on the *Irish Examiner* sports desk for their help and support; to the nice people in O'Brien's coffee shop in Douglas Village Shopping Centre, who've always looked after me, Clara and Bridget, whenever we land in; and to Lil and Michael Downey and family for everything they have done for Clara and Bridget over the years.

Thanks to my mother Mary for stepping in whenever our ability to keep the dynamic duo under control was stretched to the limit. Nana has so much energy she'd have finished this book in half the time (something Fergal Tobin may want to note).

A mention for my Dad, Donal, who died before my first book was published. I always wanted you to see your name in one of these. You are not forgotten.

Finally, thanks to Marjorie for backing me and sending me off on so many days to talk to people, which meant she had to hold the fort alone. I appreciate it, believe me. Holding the fort means Clara and Bridget, of course: all we were ever missing was the two of you. Some day you may pick this up and see what Dad was doing all that time. Apologies in advance for the lack of talking pigs or magic cats.

INTRODUCTION

Thoughts from the Dismal Science

Unique in its voluntary ethos, an organisation dedicated to recycling any money it raises to spread the gospel of hurling and Gaelic football, handball, camogie and ladies' football, a vast, selfless family of like-minded individuals all working together for the greater good of the Association as a whole.

Or a vast, rapacious empire of warring groups and factions, each trying their best to outdo the others in order to rake in some of the enormous amounts of cash rolling around the organisation, all gathered under a veil of shamateurism and hypocrisy.

Your viewpoint probably depends on whether or not you are a card-carrying member of the Gaelic Athletic Association, but even then there are nuances. Many die-hard GAA people would be unhappy with the organisation's attitude towards money, whether that applies to ticket prices or player endorsements, funding the Gaelic Players' Association (GPA) or opening Croke Park to rugby or soccer.

With that in mind, this book looks at the tension between two realities: the GAA's sports mission, which centres on participation in amateur sport, and the financial reality that goes along with generating vast amounts of money all over the country.

First stop, then, a couple of economists.

————

John Considine lectures in the dismal science at University College Cork. He pinpoints that tension between the commercial imperative and the organisation's mission: "Nobody gets rich working for the GAA, basically. The bottom line regarding the GAA's role is games development, so as a result it engages in practices that you'd have to say in economics terms, 'you could do better.'"

Jim Power of Friends First is a well-known economic commentator across a range of media platforms, and he echoes Considine. "I think those two areas come into conflict now and again, but I don't see it as a perennial problem. Looking at All-Ireland final day or Munster final day there's no conflict whatsoever. You have a sporting occasion that gives the GAA maximum positive advertising, puts the Association in the shop window—and is totally economically viable for the GAA. The conflict comes with activities which the GAA must engage in to keep it in the shop window, or to promote games or to advertise and market games. There are some activities the GAA engages in which make no economic sense whatsoever."

Eamon O'Shea is a professor of economics at the National University of Galway who feels that tension is "generally managed well" by the GAA.

"Within the context of the GAA you have the quasi-professionalism of the game at county level, and the amateur aspect of the game everywhere else," he says. "Obviously it's quasi-professional because there's a lot of revenue generated over the summer in the championship, and from the top league games. The sustainability of that, given the current structure . . . everything's more professional now with paid physios, paid trainers, paid psychologists, paid doctors. You also have bureaucrats paid at the top end, and in between you have players and managers, and even there some managers are being paid. So that's one obvious tension.

"The other tension relates to the money generated, how that trickles down. I don't have evidence that that isn't happening, and all the evidence that is there suggests that it is—that it does trickle down—but how and where that money trickles down is an interesting question.

"There's also an interesting demographic tension in that the GAA is essentially a rural organisation which is trying to catch up with an urban demography. That's going to be very interesting in the sense of how resources are channelled, how structures are set up—even how matches are fixed. One of the obvious things is that if you fix games in urban environments you're more likely to get people to come, whereas in rural environments they have longer distances to travel—as basic as that. There's a whole raft of interesting issues like that within the GAA."

———

Okay, I cheated a little bit.

Jim Power is a well-known economist, but he is also a die-hard Waterford GAA supporter who is heavily involved in that county's supporters' club. John Considine won All-Ireland medals with Cork as a robust corner back before becoming a respected coach at all levels within his home county, serving as interim senior manager in 2009. And finally, Eamon O'Shea is a former Tipperary hurler widely regarded as one of the finest coaches in the game and generally credited with Tipperary's dazzling display of attacking hurling in their All-Ireland final victory of 2010. As the book went to press he was installed as senior hurling manager in the Premier County. Of course, if you're a GAA person you knew all of that already.

Power brings a personal resonance to the tension we mentioned within the GAA. "Where that tension happens, primarily, is with kids, and I've seen examples with my own kids," he says.

"When they got old enough they played in the Cumann na mBunscoil finals in Dublin, which every year is played in Croke Park. Now it makes no economic sense to the GAA to open up Croke Park for kids like that, but letting them out on the field there to play is something that they'll never forget. That encourages kids to go on and play Gaelic games, so it makes sense in terms of retention of kids.

"But then one year one of my sons was on the team that made it to the final, and the game had to be moved from Croke Park to Parnell Park, because there was a concert in Croke Park. The kids were unbelievably disappointed, because playing in Croke Park was the pinnacle for them, and I felt that the kids' place should not have been affected by blatant commercialism which was outside the realm of sport within the GAA.

"The GAA has to keep its focus on the product first and foremost in my view, and that's sport. The product will be more and more

successful the more people participate. I think the key for the GAA is
to get more and more people participating, as far as that's possible: if
that means turning down commercially lucrative opportunities like
concerts, I think that's a price worth paying. Concerts come and go,
but get a kid playing GAA and you'll have him for 20 years. Or longer."

O'Shea sees the tension breaking out in his overview of the GAA's
economic mission, and in particular its use of its resources. He feels
one of the GAA's biggest challenges, for instance, is in coming to
terms with the actuality of urban life.

"Look at a place like Knocknacarra, where I live in Galway. There
are 10,000 to 12,000 people there and I don't think the GAA is tapping
into that resource fully. The structures set up to generate competition
within these areas . . . rather than having one superclub, if you had
several small clubs feeding into one elite club, but in general I don't
think the GAA understands the dynamic of urban living, of urban
choices, or the priorities of families when it comes to pastimes,
priorities which are very different to families in rural areas.

"I think the GAA is only playing catch-up in that context in terms of
organisational frameworks and supports. Dublin has been successful
in developing hurling because it recognised the need for facilities, for
floodlit hurling, to structure the games in order to have consistent
matches and all of that. I don't know if that's the case in counties
which are dominated by a rural landscape and a rural ideology."

For his part, Considine crystallises the tension within the GAA
by using the example of supporters' clubs, and how those function
with counties, for instance, in comparison with professional sports
organisations.

"I don't see any downside in supporters' clubs unless they're taking
money from the county board itself, and I couldn't see that happening.
The funny thing is that for a professional outfit a supporters' club is
a bit of a drain, while in the GAA they're there to help the sports
team. On balance I think most people see them as more positive than
negative."

Considine dwells further on the GAA person's double-think: "As
an economist I don't favour tax breaks for GAA players, for instance,
because they're not mobile. The point in giving the horse-racing

industry tax breaks is to encourage owners to keep their horses in Ireland. That's not the case with the GAA players' tax break. As a person who likes sport, though, there's a part of me that says, why shouldn't sports people get a piece of the action; everyone else is. And as an individual GAA person, if you gave me the choice of playing an All-Ireland in front of 100,000 fans and a million on TV, or in front of nobody, I'd take the former."

Okay. You've paid your money and the ball's been thrown in. Enjoy the game.

PART ONE: CASH FLOW

Chapter 1 ∿

THE SIGNIFICANCE OF 80 PER CENT: THE BOTTOM LINE

This is what the GAA brings in. The 2011 season, the last year for which figures were available, showed an overall drop in revenue of €11 million, down from €58m in 2010 to €47m in 2011, but the decrease was foreseen and planned for and could in part be attributed to the loss in revenue—€4m—from the rental of Croke Park to the FAI and the IRFU in 2010.

Gate receipts from Central Council games showed a drop of €2m, attributed to price reductions and the International Rules Series being played in Ireland the previous year, while attendances at championship games were down by just 2 per cent.

The average attendance at championship matches in the All-Ireland series showed a minimal decline, dropping from a 2010 average of 16,900 to 16,300 in 2011, while total attendances for Central Council games rose by 10 per cent at €1.2m.

Revenue from GAA football championship games was down by 10 per cent, while income from the GAA hurling championship increased by 4 per cent; attendances in the Allianz Football and Hurling Leagues increased to 369,000 in 2011, with revenues growing by €0.7m to €3.5m, with the Dublin Spring Series, which was played at Croke Park, driving that increase.

A decrease of €4.5m in commercial revenue to €15.2m was down to ten fewer Championship matches being shown live on TV in 2011 and the shorter reporting period, 1 January 2011 to 31 October, as opposed to the full calendar year in 2010. At the same time, indirect costs dropped by €1.3m to €6.7m and the costs of staging competitions and matches fell by €1m.

Finally, approximately 80 per cent of all revenues was recycled directly to other units within the Association, with Central Council distributing €37m in funding during 2011, while there was an investment of €9m in games development. "When you take a number of factors into account," said Tom Ryan, the GAA financial director, "around 86 per cent of the revenue that people pay at the turnstiles when they go to see a match is recycled within the Association."

A few months after his presentation of the figures, Ryan settles down to give an overview of the GAA's finances. "Recent years were probably distorted by the soccer and rugby games in Croke Park. In terms of funding the GAA works off gate receipts, sponsorship, broadcasting money, State funding and business activities within the stadium (Croke Park), but the first three are the big ones in terms of scale. Attendances have held stable, but the money we make out of that is dropping because of price reductions, season tickets, packages— and that's not an accident. We'd have deliberated on that and decided that it was important to keep people in the habit of going to games. In marketing terms it's far easier to keep people than it is to win them back.

"When you think of the couple of million attendances at games over the course of the year, I don't know if we can tell exactly whether that's a smaller number of people going to more matches. That means if you lose a few people it can have an exponential effect on attendances.

"I accept there are any number of costs on top of ticket prices, too. If you have kids you're familiar with the experience of bringing them to a game with €60 in your pocket and when you get home that's gone, and you're not sure where it went. Because of those costs,

I'm not sure if cutting ticket prices further would have much of an impact. For instance, we cut the prices of early-round games last year compared to the latter end, but our figures show that attendances are good later compared to those early games. That isn't done solely to boost attendances, though; without sounding corny, it's genuinely being fair to people, because if their county makes it to an All-Ireland semi-final it could be their third or fourth outing of the summer. Out of fairness to them, it doesn't cost us a huge deal to take a fiver off the ticket price for a first round game."

That economic driver for the GAA—bums on seats—is viewed by Ryan as the "best barometer for everything else". You've got to keep them, as he says. Not only will you turn off your own consumers pretty quickly if you mess up, the other revenue streams feed directly from the atmosphere provided by big crowds.

"The number going has held up pretty okay, but it's a hard job to keep the equilibrium there. Certainly you'd be worried if we got something wrong in that regard, say, in terms of prices, venues or competition structure, that what you'd lose would be difficult to get back. That can happen. People can recall sports that were very popular in terms of spectators—snooker was huge when I was in school, but I couldn't name three top snooker players now.

"People want to go to games—you only have to look at the early-season competitions, the O'Byrne Cup or the Waterford Crystal or whatever. The weather's not great and you have lads playing that you may not see in the county jersey again, but people want to get out to see the games. You can't be cynical about that, and if you took advantage of that financially with people, while you might benefit for maybe a year or so, you could do a lot of damage. All the other stuff is directly related to the games: sponsors wouldn't be interested, for instance, if the stadium is half-empty. Neither would broadcasters. So a lot hinges on attendances."

And here the tension between the economic imperative and the GAA's games promotion objective comes into view. Ryan admits that when he watches the championship draws in the autumn, he's doing a little mental arithmetic at the same time. "Even in the 2013 championship draw you'd have half an eye on the financial return:

you'd have Cork-Kerry in the football in Munster, a good opening game in the Ulster championship—that kind of thing—even if it's not the way you should be watching the championship draw."

Hang on a second, though. If you're the GAA's financial chief, surely it's incumbent on you to view those fixtures through the prism of your day job, even if that sums up the tension between the day job and the fan's interest in the games coming down the line? "Tension's a good way to put it because there are a lot of inherent contradictions. The whole thing is volunteer led and community based, and we're not here to make a profit, but at the same time if you started work on a Monday morning thinking, sure it doesn't matter if we make a surplus or not, you wouldn't be around too long. If we were all *laissez-faire* it wouldn't work, because everything we're trying to do needs resources. Money. We have to find a balance between making a profit and keeping true to your ideals, and what you're there for."

That sounds like a professional approach with a small 'p'; later in the book Dessie Farrell of the GPA says the GAA will need to be professional in its approach to preserve its amateur ethos, and Ryan acknowledges the point.

"If you interpret professionalism as running things properly, in the right way, then that's the way everything has to be run, down to your own club, never mind the GAA as a whole. That's a world away from professionalism as many people understand the term, but it's a good discipline for the GAA to have.

"For instance, if you were interviewing people for a job in Croke Park, it's nice if the successful candidate has an interest in the games— and most of them do—but you wouldn't be doing the GAA a service if you awarded the job to the biggest hurling fan you interviewed rather than the best-qualified accountant, for instance.

"The other side of that is that you can find yourself telling GAA people how to run things, and these are people whose spare time, whose family time, is being affected by their voluntary work, and you can sense there may be a little gap between Croke Park and the club man. It's something I'd love to get rid of."

There are other issues he'd like to address. When the ticket price for the 2012 All-Ireland hurling final replay was cut from €80 to €50, it meant the excitable prediction of a €5 million windfall from that replay had to be revised downwards. Not that they were accurate to begin with, he says. "It wouldn't be anything like that, even before you factor in price reductions for tickets and so on," says Ryan. "An All-Ireland final is worth—purely in terms of admissions and tickets—about €4 million. When you cut prices, as we did for the replay, then the gross out of the replay is about €2.5 million. There's a big cost in running it. There are plenty of expenses involved, and at the end there's €1.5 million to €2 million out of a replay. Now it's great to have, and it's obviously not something I'd ever complain about, but in realistic terms it's not going to transform everyone's fortunes overnight."

And in terms of that old urban legend of GAA referees being under orders to create lucrative draws? "People have this kind of notion that referees play for draws, something that's died out a little in recent years but which was suggested for years. You've had plenty of one-point games in the last few years which disproved that, and I think the figures show that on average there are only two draws a year in the big inter-county games. To be fair, I think you tend to hear that only from people who have little or no interest in Gaelic games, so it's not as if it's worth engaging in; anyone with even a passing familiarity with hurling or football doesn't really buy into that.

"But even with our own constituency we have to lay out what we expect to make and what we intend to do with that—if only to temper people's expectations. Otherwise people would think 'this is open season.'"

For all that, Ryan doesn't detect much Grab-All-Association cynicism directed towards the GAA these days.

"I don't, really. I think—I'd like to think—that there's a perception out there that we run things okay. But I think we can be a little paranoid about that kind of thing ourselves. One thing we can say is that coming from my background, preparing accounts and presenting them, so far, the GAA is the most transparent place I've ever been. It has to be, because it's nobody's money except the general membership.

"The other side of that, though, is that it's not what most people are interested in. The figures are published *ad nauseam*, but whether people trawl through them all, I don't know. That's not a reason not to publish them, and you'd hear at times about how other sports treat their figures, but that's not something that I think we should be doing, measuring ourselves against other sports. You're good at what you do. You stand on your own merits and they are the best games in the world and so on. If you believe in what you're doing, then it doesn't matter what anybody else is doing or saying.

"To be honest, it's something that annoys me at times about Irish life in general—not just the GAA—this constant looking over the shoulder at what the English are saying about us, or what these other people are saying about us. Why should we care? Everything we bring in is accounted for. If we give a club €50, it's down in black and white. The truth is that that can be a head-wrecker, preparing accounts to that level of detail, but it's also something to be proud of, to be open to that level of scrutiny.

"At every Congress we'll spend two or three hours going through the figures with people and I accept that that's not the most scintillating topic. I appreciate that, but it's important to be able to say that you do that."

Of course, the fact that members of the media wouldn't be the most numerate with lengthy balance sheets isn't a help. "That's the way of the world," he says. "My own interests are in Gaelic games and you could say that what I'm doing is a poor substitute for what I'd like to be doing games-wise!

"I don't expect people to slaver over the numbers; I know that what we do is the kind of thing that only gets headlines when it goes wrong, frankly. If it goes okay then nobody's that interested, which is fine by me."

Chapter 2 ⌒

THE GREAT SECRET SPRINGTIME REVENUE GENERATOR

One of Tom Ryan's parting comments is about the national leagues, which is surprising. When it comes to less attractive siblings, the national leagues leave the ugly sisters in the ha'penny place.

Grim locations, small crowds, bad weather. Every year it yields a nice end-of-year photograph or two, and that's about it: a few stewards wrapping frozen fingers around mugs of tea, or a couple of hardy souls huddling from a hailstorm under an underused scoreboard. All that remains of a dismal Sunday afternoon.

Even the managers and players can barely hide their true feelings about the competition. The expression 'league is league, championship is championship' rotates heavily in the early months of the year, with a heavy bias towards the attractiveness of the championship. If teams make it to the semi-finals, fair enough. They'll try to kick on and collect a medal, but by the same token, almost every year a couple of sides 'train through' and abandon any pretence at competitiveness as long as they're not relegated. Every now and again a couple of counties will forget themselves and serve up a private exhibition of high scoring that leads to a brief ripple of optimism, but seasonal torpor and the fact that many long-serving players take a springtime break from the treadmill ahead of the grounds hardening usually reasserts itself.

Despite all of that, county boards try everything to get the crowds through the turnstiles. Free entry for kids, ticket packages, marching bands, pop groups—see Dublin's innovative Spring Series, which featured Jedward at half-time one year, which certainly lowered the average age of those in attendance—but people refuse to love the league, it seems. The visual contrast between the grey terraces speckled with hardy souls in anoraks and the shirt-sleeved multitudes baking under the championship sun can't be overstated.

Oddly enough, they should. Because, as Tom Ryan said, it's good news financially for their county after all.

———

It was a run-of-the-mill press call in Nowlan Park, where Kilkenny were extending their association with Glanbia and Avonmore.

Brian Cody and some of his players were present and one of them, Jackie Tyrrell, pinpointed the attraction of the league for administrators when asked about a new six-team format. On the playing side it meant few games for managers to try out new players and Tyrrell, one of the more thoughtful players around, threw out some boiler-plate about managers being less keen to take risks with selection as a result. Then he added, as an afterthought: "If you look at it from a county board's perspective it's less revenue." Tyrrell was correct. County boards don't like seeing any revamp of league structures which means fewer games, because it hits their bottom line.

John Considine managed the Cork senior hurlers for a couple of league games before returning to the Department of Economics in UCC. He points out that county boards do better out of the drudgery of the league than the dazzle of the championship. "You get a greater return for the league games than you do for championship games. Munster final revenue goes to the Munster Council and the same in other provinces, while All-Ireland final revenue is redistributed around the Association."

But how does that break down? While writing this book a resurgent Cork, under returning icon Jimmy Barry-Murphy, played Waterford in front of a crowd of over 7,000 in the hurling league. Ger Lane of the Cork County Board crunched the numbers. "Well, it doesn't go to the county board directly from the game," says Lane. "The county board gets a fee for hosting the game and the rest is pooled with all the other gates for the league, and whatever the total is, you get a percentage refunded: in 2011 our accounts showed Cork's share to be €120,000 approximately from both hurling and football.

"It's one of the biggest revenue generators for county boards. Take the Munster championship. You get a flat fee to cover your expenses for the game unless you're hosting it, in which case you get a fee for renting the stadium. That's a major source of finance as can be seen in our annual accounts—€180,000 in 2011, while it was €340,000 in 2010 when we hosted extra games. People wonder why county boards are so keen on hosting games, and that's why. It's a lucrative business. If Cork were playing Kerry in Fitzgerald Stadium in the football championship, and playing hurling in Thurles, then obviously we'd benefit far more from the league games, as the venues benefit largely in championship games."

That may not quite fit with the image of thousands of supporters converging on a provincial final or semi-final, but it explains why county boards love the league, if nobody else does. It also goes some way to explaining county boards' interest in the sharp end of the league. "It's why counties are always very keen on progressing to the semi-finals and finals of the national leagues, as the bigger the attendance the more the county gets in gate returns from headquarters," adds Lane.

"We beat Dublin in the league final last year, and that's the kind of opposition everybody wants, because they'll fill Croke Park and consequently the percentage of the gate is very valuable. In general terms the income for the 7,000 people you might have at a national league game would be greater than the income for a Munster championship game in Thurles, say, where you're bringing maybe 20,000 Cork supporters to Semple Stadium and you get a few thousand euro to cover your team costs. The money generated at Munster Championship games does come back to clubs by way of grants, by the way. It doesn't come back into the county board accounts, but 37 Cork clubs received over €325,000 in 2011, and money redistributed to Munster clubs over the last five years is in excess of €7.5 million."

Laudable, but isn't there one potential problem here? Surely when it's more profitable for a county board to progress in the league there's a temptation for the county board to put pressure on the manager to win games when he might want to use some of those games for experimentation in selection? "The potential exists," says Lane, "but in my time involved, while privately board members might say 'that's not a very strong team going out today', there wouldn't be a case where a member would influence the manager—nor would a manager accept it. We appoint the management and we stand by that. And of course you also have the case nowadays that most teams want to make the knock-out stages because they can see there's a benefit to the team later on in the championship."

There's another twist to the attitude to the national league. Why don't some counties move games out of the big county grounds to maximise attendance? Wouldn't they draw bigger crowds at some smaller venues and get more money, a better atmosphere and a better chance of winning the game in question?

"I'd love to see Cork play a league game in Mallow, or in Clonakilty," says Lane. "My understanding is each county must name three county venues suitable for hosting inter-county games and in our case those would be the two stadiums we have in the city, Pairc Uí Chaoimh and Pairc Uí Rinn, and Fermoy."

Yet some counties see an obvious benefit in utilising less central venues, to put it politely. The usual example cited here is Monaghan, and as a liaison officer with the Cork senior footballers, Lane is familiar with the backroads of Patrick Kavanagh country.

In many counties, visiting teams are often brought out to rural grounds, and nobody would be surprised if the county board had done some kind of deal with the venue for the rent. To many observers it makes sense to have a couple of games brought to the people, rather than the public being asked to come to the city. A couple of years ago

Liverpool drew 7,000 people to Dunmanway for a soccer game, for example, and many observers on Leeside believe that if an intercounty league game in Mallow or Clonakilty were properly marketed, that it would draw the same type of crowd, never mind the inevitable promotion dividend for the game in that area. Venues vary widely. One observer who has accompanied the Cork senior football team on many journeys around the country points out that they've been to some venues around the country which look positively shabby in comparison with the Mallow GAA club complex, for instance. All of that without taking into consideration the inevitable benefit to the home side of playing a game in an environment hostile to the visiting team. Anyone who's been to Scotstown in Monaghan when the supporters there are clung up to the wire will acknowledge that their presence in that setting was worth something to the Monaghan team.

There's also a little-known but potentially enriching sideline when it comes to hosting games, one which could be used to sweeten the deal needed to facilitate a game being moved away from the main county ground. Elsewhere in this book you can read about the future of match-day information, the possibility of downloadable apps which will inform you of team selections, but in the meantime . . .

"Don't forget, by the way, the venue could make a lot of money out of the programme sales alone," says Lane. "That's very lucrative. That's worth a lot. If you had 5,000 people at a game you'd sell 2,000 programmes and that would earn €4,000 to €5,000 for the venue. Programmes earn a lot of money. The City Division of the GAA in Cork has been stood down, but they had made serious money over the years—all hard earned—from programme sales. You could produce a programme for 50 to 75 cent a copy and sell it for €2: there's a big profit margin. The rule of thumb is generally that you'd sell one programme to every third spectator, but that can change with a smaller event. Why is that? A junior or intermediate county final between two teams who've never reached that level before, or rarely, then you'd sell programmes to two in every three spectators because they'd want a souvenir of the occasion. You'd often have people even coming along afterwards looking for programmes for that reason."

Considine, speaking from experience, concurs with Lane on the issue of pressure on managers to select teams specifically to advance to the knock-out stages of the national league. "I don't think there's a manager in the country who would care about that. If they felt playing every league game behind closed doors would help them winning the championship, they'd do it, not to mention the positives from winning league games. I'd say you wouldn't need all the fingers on one hand to count the inter-county managers who would be aware of the breakdown of league revenues per county; you wouldn't need the remaining fingers to work out how many of them cared about it. Where there could be greater pressure on generating money would be in promotion, particularly with counties with supporters' clubs. There could potentially be pressure on players turning up to meet sponsors and so on, though I've not heard of that happening."

So managers are like the rest of us: resistant to the league's dubious charms. It looks like it'll have to keep relying on that small audience, county board treasurers all over Ireland, to make up its fan club.

Chapter 3 ~

THE PA DILLON-BOB DYLAN CONUNDRUM: CONCERT REVENUE

The collision between cutting-edge music and the GAA, in terms of concerts held in GAA grounds, has provided some handy copy for journalists over the years. It's not so very long ago that Bob Dylan was due to play Nowlan Park, Kilkenny, and the then-county board chairman was asked for his views on the sixties troubadour. "Ah, I'd be more of a Pa Dillon man myself," said the chairman, referencing the Kilkenny defender who created an environment around the small square in Nowlan Park that was a good deal more hostile than the mellow vibe engendered by Bob's musical stylings.

Then there was the time that Prince was bringing his purple self to Pairc Uí Chaoimh back in 1990. When it was explained to a member of the Cork County Board that the little man's stage show was on the raunchy side, the reaction was immortal: "We are going to have to sit down around the table with Prince and discuss this."

They never did, which is unfortunate on every level you can think of, obviously. If they had to meet nowadays, though, there's every chance that Prince would use the very thing which has hurt the GAA concert concept more than anything. The M8.

———

One of the men involved in Siamsa Cois Laoi sketched the commercial background to that short-lived musical festival for us under strict conditions of anonymity.

"There was a particular arrangement that time under which the venue owners were guaranteed their cut no matter how many came along," he said. "That was obviously very attractive at the time, and maybe it's something you could hammer out in a deal even now, but something that militates against doing something similar is the quality of the road from Cork to Dublin, oddly enough.

"There was a time that road was so bad people wouldn't travel it for a midweek concert because they couldn't face driving back down again. Nowadays you're in Dublin from Cork in two hours and a bit, so it's no hardship. What that means is that people are willing to head to Dublin for a concert, and promoters know that. Why risk a band in Cork or Limerick or Galway when you can pitch the O2 or some other venue in Dublin to them and you'll get a bigger crowd?"

———

With Croke Park, stadium director Peter McKenna has a different focus. The venue may appear to have the upper hand, but it must also maintain its brand value. "Well, the promoter takes the risk. That's how we have our deal structured. Having said that, if you had a whole string of poorly attended events the whole thing would fall off very quickly. I think Croke Park is one of the top five outdoor concert venues in Europe. Everybody wants to play here. They love it; they love the atmosphere. Westlife and Take That had their concerts filmed here. Billboard voted us the number one concert venue in the world after the U2 shows. So we're up there.

"Only a handful of bands will fill the stadium, but we'll only look for a handful of bands. We have a pre-eminent position for concerts. They work well; we do it well; the quality of the facilities, the ease of getting in and out; the sheer size of the place. That all ties in together and everyone comments on it, saying Croke Park is number one. Slane, Lansdowne—none of them comes close."

There's one little-known factor which can affect the bands playing in Croke Park. In testimony reminiscent of the Cork County Board's interest in hauling Prince before its General Purposes Committee, McKenna admits that the GAA has the power of vetoing acts or bands. "We would have a veto if we thought the act was unsuitable. We've never had to use that and I couldn't imagine the circumstances in which we'd have to use it. The promoter, effectively, comes to us and says, this is what I've got lined up, we agree dates, and it takes off from there. Twenty years ago some acts might have been on the edge, but not now. I couldn't see that being an issue. We do insist on having an Irish act on the bill, mind you, as we see ourselves as promoting Irish music."

———

For the GAA outside the capital the pickings are a bit slimmer because they're in a Catch-22 situation. On the face of it a middle-ranking act or two might fill a stadium like Salthill or Walsh Park, but for stadiums like the Gaelic Grounds or Thurles you're talking about a band or singer who can pull 50,000 people through the gates.

"There's more to that than meets the eye, though we're exploring this option with the Gaelic Grounds," says Enda McGuane, then deputy CEO of the Munster Council. "Timing has a lot to do with it. The need for finance within the GAA is greater because of the decline in revenue from other sources, obviously, but the difficulty is that concerts are now being hit as well. Advance sales are under pressure.

"If you go back three years you had a huge festival like Oxegen which might sell out in 35 minutes as soon as the tickets went online. That doesn't happen any more. We see it ourselves. We see that people won't buy tickets well in advance because they want to wait and see if they have the cash to go to the gig—or if there is a cheaper option that weekend. So concerts aren't as viable as they were a couple of years ago.

"The other thing to bear in mind is that the level of expertise needed to run concerts has moved on hugely. Structures have changed and the days of guaranteed money are gone. It's not as lucrative as it used to be, and you're also handing over the management of the event to an outside agency. By their nature the acts you're looking to bring in are international acts, so you're going to have to go through a promoter, which will hit your costs."

There's also the small matter of the people who live near the stadium. As McGuane puts it, they may be willing to tolerate the occasional crowd filing past their front gates on their way to a hurling or football game, but thousands of drunken teenagers present a different threat to the prize rose bushes in the front garden.

"There's the planning, and people's willingness, or lack of same, to accommodate it. It's one thing for people who live near a stadium to have a game for a couple of hours with some cheering the odd time on a Sunday afternoon or Wednesday evening, but it's another thing to have it all day. People mightn't be as willing to accommodate that. And that would probably be an issue anywhere. Once people hear about concerts and kids running riot, they'll think, 'Well, do we want that?'"

And if you lose the goodwill of your neighbours, that can be a huge problem down the line, as anyone with a misconceived house extension can tell you. Even when you decide to take a punt you need your wits about you, which the Waterford County Board discovered in the summer of 2012.

They went for broke, advertising a Rhythm Fest in Dungarvan in an attempt to drum up funds for board activities. Clearly they thought they had a winner with Jedward, who entertained crowds at one of the Dublin Spring Series games, but the event, spread over two days, was poorly attended.

The disappointment wasn't confined to merchants in the Dungarvan area: estimates of the losses suffered by the Waterford County Board ranged from €30,000 to €50,000, but one precaution might have helped the Déise officials with their planning.

The Rhythm Fest was down for the weekend of 30 June, but Jedward had already played in Tramore on 3 June, ensuring that anyone from the east of the county who wanted to see them would hardly make the trip to Dungarvan a few weeks later.

Critics might say that if the Waterford County Board officials had been more conversant with the schedules of the big pop sensations they'd have been able to take precautions to protect their big gig, but you can't expect the people running hurling and football in a county to be followers of music as well, can you?

Chapter 4 ⌒

THE NAME ABOVE THE DOOR: STADIUM NAMING

Elsewhere in this book Peter McKenna pours cold water on the prospect of Croke Park selling naming rights to parts of the stadium such as the Hogan Stand, and with good reason.

The stadium director isn't just paying lip service to a notional interest in history among GAA members, but recognising that there are some measures that won't wash. No matter how persuasive the economic arguments in their favour, the Association's membership won't stand for certain developments.

The other side of that debate isn't long being aired by those in units of the GAA elsewhere in the country, however: namely, that it's all very well for the biggest stadium in the country to remove itself from the naming-rights debate when revenue isn't a challenge, in real terms, for that venue. What about other venues in the country, those which don't have full houses guaranteed half a dozen times a year? Can they afford to keep their names uncluttered by advertising slogans or catchy jingles?

———

Mick O'Keeffe of Pembroke Communications can see both sides of the argument, but he finesses the question a little. Some places have strong identities already. What happens with a new build? Can you reinvent the venue?

"Go to America. Most of the big grounds have company names attached. There's an element of saturation involved, and the way Aviva's corporate business has gone, things have soured a little in terms of naming rights. When it's a new build, or a re-build, you've a chance to break with the past, but given the history and traditions associated with Pairc Uí Chaoimh, for instance, would renaming that as O2 Park sit well with people in Cork? If there were a few million euro going into grass-roots GAA then it might. I think Cork have a chance, with such a big, prestigious stadium, to sell naming rights. But you want to get the company in for five to ten years."

O'Keeffe can offer examples of venues which renamed successfully—not all of them sports venues, either. "Parnell Park is another case. From a promoting the game perspective the Spring Series has been a success, but there can be times when Croke Park is a bit lonely during a league game. I think 20,000 is about the bottom number for atmosphere in Croke Park, otherwise it's terrible, and we've had 25,000 there for the Spring Series, but a 25,000-seater stadium would be perfect for Dublin GAA. You'd fill it for most national league games. You'd have a good atmosphere and it'd be an opportunity to get money for naming rights. And the name would stick if you're in it for the long haul. Don't forget, our generation would remember the Point Theatre, but kids of 15 and 16 only know it as the O2 and only refer to it as the O2. So it can stick."

Further south, Enda McGuane can identify a couple of examples of naming rights away from Croke Park which have recently come on stream: "You have Kingspan Breffni Park in Cavan, while Glennon Brothers Pearse Park is the ground in Longford.

"It's interesting. You don't hear a lot of people saying Lansdowne Road any more, it's mostly the Aviva people refer to. It's an obvious stream of revenue, and there are a lot of those streams which the GAA hasn't explored, some of which just wouldn't fit with the organisation.

"The GAA a lot of the time is skirting a line between professional sport and the fact that it's a not-for-profit organisation, and you can't be as hard-headed as other organisations. Otherwise you'd say naming rights were a no-brainer. But at the same time Old Trafford is still Old Trafford, and that's the most commercially driven organisation in a professional, commercially driven sport."

———

Incidentally, some of the "other streams" referred to by McGuane may become available sooner rather than later. It may seem a little early to be looking a decade down the track at what other sports may be working on, but McGuane recognises the Rugby World Cup in 2023 as a potential opportunity for the GAA. GAA President Liam O'Neill has summed up the GAA's situation regarding any bid for that tournament neatly, saying the GAA can't guarantee the success of a bid, but can guarantee its failure if it doesn't make venues available.

However, McGuane distinguishes between once-off events like the Rugby World Cup and throwing open GAA club pitches all over Ireland. "Look at the amount of money the GAA has poured into infrastructure for decades. It's huge.

"One thing about New Zealand that struck me when I was there was the fact that every little village had a set of rugby posts, the way every little village in Ireland has GAA goalposts. Sometimes you see a little stand, or floodlights, and you'd nearly ask where the team is that'd use them.

"That's one reason I distinguish between club grounds and major stadiums. The simple reason is that a lot of voluntary effort went into the former, and the reality is that it wouldn't be practical to open up those grounds to general use by other sports. If a soccer or rugby team were using a GAA club's pitch all winter and you tried to play hurling on it come the spring or summer, it wouldn't work. The resources to maintain the pitch to the required standard wouldn't exist in many clubs."

Going on to the major venues, it's clear that there are 26 stadiums with a capacity of over 20,000 in Ireland, and the GAA owns 23 of those. The reality is, however, that only Croke Park and Semple Stadium have the potential to be self-financing.

"You then have a situation where grounds like Pairc Uí Chaoimh, Cusack Park, the Gaelic Grounds—fantastic stadiums all around the country, but they don't have the capacity to generate the revenue to sustain themselves. So you look at the prospect of opening up stadiums on a once-off basis or, looking ahead, to an issue that's coming down the road, the Rugby World Cup in 2023. If Ireland put in a bid, is the GAA going to come on board with that? From a financial perspective it makes eminent sense because you'd open it once or twice a year and then have the pitch in pristine condition when you need it for your own games during the summer.

"There's a cultural issue in the sense that people would put forward the argument that you're promoting alternative sports, but the reality is those games are going to be played anyway. In the case of the Rugby World Cup, would it be worse to have Ireland lose out on the opportunity to host that tournament? That's something that'll have to be addressed."

John Considine looks at the opening grounds conundrum from another angle. "I think the argument against opening Croke Park was that you were opening the stadium to your competitors. If you don't make your stadium available, will that result in more people playing Gaelic games and fewer people playing rugby? I don't think so. As the GAA becomes more commercial, or professional if you want to put it that way, I don't think they can turn those opportunities down, no more than they can turn down music concerts and so on to generate revenue. If it's a one-off, a Rugby World Cup, then I think they may have to do so."

As this book was going to press, former president Seán Kelly chipped in while speaking to the *Irish Examiner*. "Obviously, Croke Park is available. Croke Park opened permanently years ago. People at the time said that would lead to an onslaught. There was no onslaught. Maybe the time has come to make a pitch or two available for special occasions in the national interest. Congress will have to approve it but as long as it is strictly for special occasions they can be judged on their merits. I would see an opportunity for the GAA, without damaging its own rules or its commitment to its own games, to look at that in a broader context."

A temporary return for rugby looks like an idea which is likely to be revived in the near future. What chances a temporary renaming for Croke Park or other venues at the same time, though?

Chapter 5 ◡

ALL THOSE BREAKFAST ROLLS ADD UP: WHAT THE GAA DOES FOR LOCAL ECONOMIES

There's one stick that's usually used against Croke Park as a match venue—or Dublin, to be more precise.

If you are in Thurles or Clones, Portlaoise or Castlebar, on the day of a big championship game, then even if you've beamed down from Mars for the occasion you're in no doubt: the big game is simply the only show in town. By contrast, it's often remarked by people visiting Dublin in September for the All-Ireland finals that it's clear the events themselves don't impact on a vast swathe of the population. It's pretty obvious that huge numbers of people on the Luas or walking O'Connell Street have no idea there's a big game on nearby. One inter-county hurler with experience of several All-Ireland finals once remarked how surreal it was to leave the team hotel that Sunday morning and to roll down streets where pedestrians hardly noticed the team bus pass by.

He offered as a striking counterpoint the situation in the smaller provincial towns, the likes of the places we mentioned earlier, where there are county supporters on hand practically from the dawn. People head to provincial finals, in particular, to sample the atmosphere and the earlier they get there to do so the better as far as they're concerned.

And what do those people need? Beer. Newspapers. Sandwiches. Mobile phone top-ups. Cigarettes. Fizzy drinks. Breakfasts, healthy and unhealthy alike. More beer, and possibly cider if it's sunny. Rosettes and scarves. Chips and burgers. Parking. Petrol. Carvery before heading home, or maybe another slab of beer for the bus journey back.

In other words, they spend. If you've been in Thurles, say, on the day of a Munster final, there's a lot of money being spent by those waiting for the throw-in at Semple Stadium, and that scene is replicated all over the country throughout the summer.

What is the presence of thousands of people for a game worth to a local economy?

————

Enda McGuane admits first of all that there aren't hard and fast rules when it comes to working out the total spend at a big championship game; some counties spend more than others when they travel, and speculation along those lines would probably unleash a fatwa for the person doing the speculating. For all that, McGuane does have some guidelines that can be relied upon.

"When it comes to calculating the effect on an economy, it's not an exact science," he says. "It couldn't be. But Bord Fáilte has different methods of calculating spending levels at an event according to whether those attending are overnight foreign tourists, for instance, or overnight domestic tourists. The figure for the latter is an average of €59, leaving out the price of a hotel bed, obviously. A day tripper at an event is estimated to spend €40 in the place where the event is held, and that's the rate I've used, because outside of Dublin that's probably the most common way people attend GAA games."

Even then there can be fluctuations, depending on local custom. For instance, there's a tradition of people making a weekend of it when certain counties are involved, even if the distances involved don't suggest that overnighting it makes much sense.

"That's probably underestimating it somewhat. Take a Munster football final held in Fitzgerald Stadium in Killarney. You probably have 7,000–8,000 people in attendance who've booked into hotels and guesthouses the night before. There's an anomaly there in the sense that although Cork is only an hour back the road from Killarney and you wouldn't normally expect people to spend the night in a place only an hour away, Cork people have been making a weekend of the Munster football final down there for years. So that game is obviously worth significantly more than the day tripper amount would suggest."

The secondary competitions can be of even more proportional benefit, says McGuane. We're all guilty of taking the senior championships into consideration and forgetting the others, but they also set the tills ringing—and in smaller towns too.

"The U21 championships and club championships draw significant crowds as well," says McGuane. "Take a Munster junior or intermediate club championship game, a lot of which are played in Mallow because it's a central location for Munster counties and has a fine club complex that's just the right size for a club crowd. If you have 2,000 people, say, at one of those games, then multiply that by €40 and suddenly there's over €80,000 in the local economy. You could also argue that it has a greater effect within that economy because somewhere like Mallow is obviously a smaller and more concentrated economy than places like Cork or Killarney.

"We've worked with Fáilte Ireland in the last few years, selling match tickets in the Fáilte Ireland offices—the idea being that with people maybe not having the money for foreign holidays, or not as much, you could have a guy from Donegal, say, who's in Cork on holidays with the family, and if Cork were playing Kerry in Pairc Uí Chaoimh in the Munster football championship he'd probably be interested in going."

McGuane feels it's an accomplishment the GAA should be doing more to publicise. Not just the summer splurge on breakfast rolls and cheap beer: the outlay by GAA clubs all over the country on an ongoing basis, one that keeps money circulating through the economies of relatively remote areas.

"From a GAA perspective it's something we should trumpet more, the spending done by the Association. That's not just big match days in Killarney or Thurles either, by the way. Consider this. On average a GAA club costs €50,000 per year to run, even a small club. That's the cash flow. There are 570 clubs in Munster, so multiply that and you get €28.5 million. That's a huge contribution to the economy. It's payment to doctors and physios, jobs as groundsmen, purchase of fencing materials, sandwiches from the local shop, paint, PA hire, laundry bills, security systems. Everything."

The flow of cash into the economy doesn't stop with clubs buying ham and bread for sandwiches either. Further up the GAA's food chain there are other commitments. "When you're talking about the outlay on grounds development and so on there's a huge contribution being made as well," he adds. "In Munster alone, despite the recession, between €25 and €26 million was spent in the last couple of years on development works—that's gone straight into construction, building dressing-rooms and so on, so it's a straight injection into an industry that's been decimated by the recession. Building supplies stores, quarries—they've all benefited. The GAA's obviously a part of society and it's also having an impact on that society."

Warming to his theme, McGuane spreads the benefits beyond the cash register.

"There's a social dividend. Of course there is. We're trying to quantify that, specifically the investment in coaches and games. We spend several million per year on coaching courses and projects and we're trying to specify the value of that to the Exchequer. Obviously there's an intangible aspect to that which you can't tie down— the well-being of a kid or the sense of development they get from participating in a game, the way it builds character and so on—but there are aspects to that which we're trying to measure.

"The Irish Heart Foundation has said 22 per cent of under-10s are obese, and if the GAA is keeping kids active in sport through their teen years, then there's a dividend down the line in terms of well-being in society as a whole. That's true of all sports, obviously, but there's a difference in Ireland compared to other countries. In France, for example, there's huge investment in sport which is controlled by the State, but here the major investment in sport is through the major sporting bodies over the last 50 to 100 years."

What are those bottom line facts and figures regarding McGuane's Bord Fáilte measurement system, then?

In 2010, the biggest game in the Munster championships, hurling and football, in terms of attendance, was the clash of Cork and Tipperary in the first round (hurling). It drew 36,827 to Pairc Uí Chaoimh and generated €1,473,080 in the local economy. The smallest show in town was Waterford versus Clare in the first round of the football championship, which drew 2,269 people to Dungarvan and put €90,760 into the local economy there. The 2010 figures are boosted somewhat by the fact that the Munster hurling final between Cork and Waterford went to a replay, as did the football semi-final that featured Cork and Kerry. In the former case, the first game drew 35,975 to Thurles and the second brought 22,763 to the replay (held on a Saturday night). All told, those two games put €2,349,000 into the coffers of the Tipperary town: a huge cash injection for a town of around 8,000 people.

The two big football games generated plenty of revenue as well. The first game in Killarney had 35,786 in attendance, and the replay in Cork was seen by 23,486 people. That drawn game put €1,431,440 into circulation in Killarney and the replay generated €939,440 in Cork.

In 2011, the last year for which figures were available, attendances held up pretty well: the biggest game was the football decider between Cork and Kerry in Killarney, with 40,892 present and spending €1,635,680; the second biggest was Cork and Tipperary in Thurles, which saw €1,249,240 spent by 31,231 spectators.

That's not the entire story, obviously. In 2010 the five games played in the Munster hurling championship drew 120,231 spectators who generated €4,809,240 in revenue. The six games in the football championship attracted 94,185 fans who spent €3,757,400. That's a total of €8,566,640.

With one game fewer in the 2011 series the numbers are proportionately lower—93,821 hurling spectators spending €3,752,840 and 64,043 football fans spending €2,561,720. But that still totals out at €6,314,560.

More than respectable when you realise, as Enda McGuane says, that those are necessarily conservative figures, and don't take into account the whole raft of games played beneath them, minor, U21 and junior or intermediate inter-county games and the club championships across the junior, intermediate and senior grades.

Multiply that by Connacht, Leinster and Ulster and you get an idea of the sheer torrent of money put into the Irish economy every year. Before we leave this area, though, one point—the 2010 provincial finals in Munster both went to draws, and both replays were particularly lucrative for the GAA.

What about that suggestion that the GAA enjoys extra revenue because its referees settle for draws if championship games are tight coming down the final furlong? That's a question you could only ask a referee, but you'll just have to wait for the answer.

PART TWO: PREMISES

Chapter 6 ∽

BROADWAY AND WALL STREET IN ONE: CROKE PARK'S VALUE TO THE GAA

I t is the enduring image of the GAA, a massive stadium rearing out of the north Dublin skyline, visible for miles in the capital.

The redevelopment of Croke Park between 1995 and 2005 from the atmospheric but dank cavern of the eighties into the dazzling palace of the twenty-first century is the ultimate trump card for GAA supporters in any intra-sport slagging. The size of the pitch seems to make the entire arena bigger, and the sheer height of the rearmost seats in the uppermost reaches of the stands took some getting used to when the stadium refurbishment was finally completed.

When rugby and soccer were finally played in the stadium while Lansdowne Road was being transformed into the Aviva, starting in 2007, there was a sense of satisfaction within the GAA at having a stadium like Croke Park at its disposal to show off to the world, but it's unlikely any GAA member felt any more validated than they had already by the admiring noises made by visiting teams and spectators. After all, if you can create Croke Park in the first place you're probably beyond the need for that kind of validation.

And if you can ensure the stadium is debt free seven years after its completion, then you're definitely beyond the need for that kind of validation.

———

Peter McKenna is the Croke Park stadium director, a forthright and articulate advocate for the ground—and for the GAA itself. McKenna is also the GAA's commercial manager, which means in some ways he embodies this book's tension in one: the ultimate guardian of the GAA's most sacred space, and the man charged with maximising the GAA's commercial presence. With that in mind, he's refreshingly frank about Croke Park's financial position.

"The figures for the stadium are in the public domain and we're probably more transparent than most PLCs in the way we present our numbers. Croke Park is debt free. All the money borrowed to build the stadium has been paid back. Approximately €62 million has been distributed back to the Association since 2006 by Croke Park and we'd have retained group revenues of maybe €90 million, so you could say that €150 million has been the bottom line in terms of revenue.

"The stadium debt is €10 million, but that's a technical debt because we have cash assets on the balance sheet of €20 million. It's a robustly healthy balance sheet and hopefully will continue to be so. We have four or five business strands—conferences, concerts, corporate boxes and matches. That Monday to Friday revenue is €3 to €4 million a year and over the next three to five years the challenge for us now is how we take a quantum step on that. Eighty per cent of what's raised is recycled through the GAA economy, as it were, so what was a massive risk when first mortgaged is now a cash cow. That's tremendous."

And yet there are other potential revenue streams. Croke Park staff need only squint out of the windows behind the Cusack Stand to see another possibility looming up on the far side of the Liffey. Wouldn't naming rights make a lot of easy money for the GAA?

McKenna pauses. "The history of the Association means people are very proud of the fact that Archbishop Croke, after whom the stadium is named, was one of the foremost figures of the time, in addition to being the GAA's first patron. And of course there are other areas within the stadium which are named for people—Michael Hogan, Michael Cusack and Maurice Davin. It would be very difficult to try to put a commercial name on top of those, and—in my view—wrong. We need to hold our history. Naming rights don't always work out successfully either. Enron named two or three stadiums in Texas and then went on to get into financial trouble due to corruption. That falls back on the stadium. I think it would be one of the last things we should ever look at, and personally I wouldn't be in favour of it. Croke Park is Croke Park, and calling it the 'X Croke Park' . . . it wouldn't work for me."

Cynics would no doubt point to the fact that it's easy to say that when you raked in millions of euro hosting Six Nations and World Cup qualifier games in rugby and soccer, of course. The difficulty with that position is the impact that revenue had on the Croke Park debt. None at all.

———

People probably forget the details of the arrangement the GAA made with itself to accommodate soccer and rugby in the first place. McKenna hasn't.

"How significant were soccer and rugby games in paying off the debt?" he says. "It actually had no impact at all. It was part of the deal that we ring-fenced the money which came in from rugby and soccer to invest in infrastructural projects throughout the country, so the €36 million generated by soccer and rugby went into those infrastructural projects around the 32 counties. Croke Park was on a solid business basis. It didn't hasten the retirement of the debt at all."

The stadium boss can tease out the financial contribution even further. Compare the much-touted £60 million of government money put into the redevelopment of Croke Park, a figure that got a lot of airplay before the stadium was opened to soccer and rugby, with the far less-touted figure of €190 million of government money put into the redevelopment of the Aviva.

"You could focus on one number and compare one against the other, but you could also look at some other points," says McKenna. "Considering the PRSI paid to the construction team, the fact that we weren't able to claim back VAT and so on, and you could claim that there was no government funding for Croke Park, because one matches the other. That's the factual position. I'd share the view that the Association doesn't get the credit for the tremendous work it does throughout the country. Croke Park is only one part of that, but it rankles with us that we can't get the Dublin Bus tour to come by the stadium. It's phenomenal to me that that still can't be achieved.

"It rankles that we can't have park and ride on the M50, with buses in and out. That's somehow expected of ourselves. It rankles that we don't have good parking. We pay—as the Aviva does—for gardaí on match day, for the clean-up on match day. We pay massive rates . . . we're more than net contributors when it comes to bringing multi-million euro economic stimuli here, and obviously you can repeat that all over the country, anywhere big games are on. People should take stock of what the GAA does. It'll continue to be done, but it could be done with better heart if so much wasn't taken for granted."

Warming to his theme, McKenna asks a relevant question about the GAA as a whole and what it invests directly into the economy. "I'm part of the National Infrastructure committee and we've put €50 to €60 million into projects around the country in the last three years. Add that to locally collected funds. That's an economic stimulus within the country of maybe €100 million. Who else is doing that? If I had a bugbear it's that I don't think the Association gets the recognition it deserves—richly deserves—in terms of the fabric of society, getting kids out, the sports, the community ethos, the volunteering. We couldn't open Croke Park on as many days without voluntary stewarding, for instance."

Sometimes you need more expertise than volunteers in Croke Park can provide, though. When you're dealing with €5,000 chickens you need professionals, as McKenna knows all too well.

But that's another story.

Chapter 7 ⤳

COMPLETING THE HORSESHOE: COVERING THE HILL AND THE FIVE GRAND CHICKEN

You couldn't call it an eyesore. Not really. But sometimes you're in the Upper Cusack or wherever your ticket takes you, and whatever way you look over to the goal on your right you see the open sky beyond the Hill, the red-and-tan rooftops of Dublin's northside stretching away and you wonder for a split-second: what would it be like if the upper stands carried all the way around Croke Park? What if there were no gap over the Hill?

Peter McKenna nods when you ask why it's never been done—and whether it can ever be attempted.

"There are technical issues and cultural issues. Technically, it's the north end of the stadium, and the sun is predominantly in the southern sky shining down, so any structure which might be built there would cut the light from any of the houses on Clonliffe Road behind it. That would be an almost impossible ask from a planning point of view."

Does that rule out any possibility of a structure at all? Clearly, having an active, busy rail line going almost through the premises would make it all the harder to get something—anything—built there.

"Hill 16 is on a slant. There's a diagonal cut through it, because the railway defines the boundary there. So you have the big bubble of Hill 16, which truncates into the Nally Terrace. It'd be very difficult. We did look at whether we could put up a glass structure so the light would pass through it to the houses on the Clonliffe Road, but the cost would be between €80 and €100 million. Substantial. It'd also reduce the capacity, because you'd have to put in seats, and it would also have an effect on the pitch. Hill 16 allows an air change because the air comes in off the back of Clonliffe College, so technically that would be a problem as well with the pitch maintenance."

There's also the other kind of atmosphere—less oxygenated, slightly louder. McKenna explains that they had to put their case very strongly when it came to retaining the terrace effect on the Hill.

"Culturally, we had four sessions with the planning authorities on this," says McKenna. "Convincing them—this was post-Hillsborough—that terracing was the way to go, that our games would be celebrated in a different, mixed way, was hugely important. It's crucial to the atmosphere, because the atmosphere in all-seater stadiums can be sanitised—we've seen that with Old Trafford. I see Hill 16 as like the GPO—a national icon. It's a monument in many ways and keeping it as a terrace is massively important, and as I say, technically it would be very difficult."

The keen-eyed may have clocked the passing reference in the technical discussions above about letting light through to the residents on the Clonliffe Road. As McKenna says, even if the planning objections were somehow overcome: "If you managed to get that planning permission, it would be an aggressive step in terms of the residents there."

The residents in the Croke Park area have often been at loggerheads with Croke Park over the problems caused by hundreds of thousands of spectators coming through a residential area, as well as the extensive building work and subsequent disruption during the stadium renovation. In addition, a long-running controversy over plans to demolish the old handball centre next to the stadium earned the dubious honour of being the subject of an RTÉ *Prime Time* programme.

The stadium director points out that anyone living in the area knows there's a stadium nearby (it's always been in their back gardens), but he adds detail on Croke Park's engagement with the community.

"We invest about €100,000 per year through a community fund in the local area—in schools and community projects—and that's been a huge positive in the local neighbourhood. We also have employment clauses with all our major contractors, so I'd say 60 to 70 per cent of the Fitzers staff, who provide catering in the stadium, are locals, and the same for the security company. So we are a source of employment and a source of investment in an area in which there's precious little of that nature.

"It's something we need to keep working at. We have a good relationship with the vast majority of people, though there are still centres of negativity. The controversy with the handball centre is one, but that will reach a conclusion shortly. If it takes another 12 months, so be it. We've pushed to change the way we deal with local issues, and we've got a community liaison officer now who goes out and talks to the people on a regular basis."

McKenna concedes that there are consequences for the residents when almost 100,000 people converge on a relatively small area, but he also points out that when the GAA stepped into the breach to host rugby and soccer games, they weren't always given the support they required.

"The events can be disruptive. We responded positively to government calls to open for soccer and rugby—there's no other stadium; let's keep the revenue here—but we found that local politicians walked away when you take an extra 800,000 people into the area for those games and didn't really respond with the positivity that was needed.

"We had to carry that burden for four or five years, and that was difficult. Another 800,000 people per year coming into the environs of Croke Park every year for four or five years was a massive imposition, and that needed to be discussed with locals. There should have been more of a national response to the locals on that basis, something meaningful; that's the importance of joined-up thinking. These big events are huge economic drivers and we're good at them, but you have to deliver right down to the nth degree on them. There's only so much individual venues can do."

———

Because Croke Park houses the elite cadre of GAA officials, it can come under fire from other ranks within the GAA. The phrase 'the suits in Croke Park' is rarely used in a complimentary way, and those at the top are sometimes accused of being remote from the concerns of hard-pressed small clubs, for instance, though later in this book former GAA president Nickey Brennan puts a persuasive counter-argument to such claims.

Wearing his commercial management hat McKenna might be included among those suits, but in his capacity as stadium boss he can prove that criticism is taken on board. "The attacks are few and far between, but that criticism keeps you grounded. There are no swelled heads. And the criticism in the main is fair and positive. Having worked in a PLC for many years, I think the speed and quality of decision-making in the GAA is swifter and better thought through than anywhere else. All inputs come to the fore very quickly, though there are a lot of side discussions beforehand, so the decision is well rounded."

One particular decision had to be made because it was clear that something had to be done. When companies talk about their core business they do so with an awareness that everything else radiates out from that. When McKenna talks about the most closely examined few acres of turf in Irish sport, he sounds a similar note.

"The pitch costs about €400,000 per year to maintain; if the pitch is to be replaced, that's another €600,000, so it's anywhere between half a million and a million euro per year. There are three full-time staff and it's non-stop. We've taken it to a point where it's manicured to perfection and head and shoulders above any other surface. It's taken a long time.

"You were asking about criticism and so on, and the pitch is where it is because we got our arses rightly kicked by managers, mentors, supporters until we got it right. The pressure was relentless. Croke Park is a goldfish bowl—there's nowhere to hide, so you don't really have an option other than to get it right. The pitch is a great example of the Association being in critical mode and getting the best result."

The pitch costs a lot, but if it doesn't work then the whole stadium is compromised as a sports venue. McKenna's right when he says there just isn't another option if the pitch isn't up to standard. Away from the underfoot conditions, however, he's keen to make a point about one misconception about Croke Park that has gained traction, somehow, in the popular mind. The frequently mentioned 'break-even figure', an attendance of 30,000 people in the stadium, is a neat, round figure, but completely meaningless.

"That's an urban myth. It costs between €40,000 and €120,000 to open the stadium and we often open it at a loss. The break-even figure? For the smallest game it would be €30,000, so 10,000 people paying €3 each, or 5,000 paying €6 each would cover it. There's never a month in Croke Park where we'd lose money hosting games—there'd be one (game) that would be high to balance one that's low, so we'd balance out. But the 30,000 attendance to break even? That's a myth."

They're proud of how far they've come. McKenna is bullish about the stadium's standing: "Each market brings its own driver, though the US is certainly at the forefront of media enhancement and so on. You'd look to the NHL, NBA, MLB and NFL at the leading edge in those terms. Nutrition, training regimes and so on, managers pull from everywhere, obviously, but when it comes to stadiums I think we have more to share with others, and I don't mean for that to sound big-headed."

Still, there can be expensive speed bumps that nobody sees coming. Even the people who operate the biggest stadiums in the US would be challenged by some of the odder problems McKenna and his team have faced. A game once came within an hour of being called off because a swarm of bees entered the stadium ("like a blanket, with a haze coming off it," recalls McKenna) and staff were at a loss as to how to deal with it. Eventually nature intervened. The bees simply flew off.

It wasn't that simple with the chickens.

"For France-Ireland in rugby back in 2007 there was a big issue about avian flu, and as everyone knows French rugby fans like to throw cockerels on to the pitch," says McKenna. "The Department of Agriculture said that if a cockerel thrown on the field were proved to have avian flu, then the stadium would have to be shut down for four to five weeks, given the threat to our poultry industry in Ireland. We had two vets on duty for the France game and three cockerels were confiscated—and put down humanely, no twisting of necks—and the bodies sent off for testing. The tests were negative, but we had the cost of the vets, the injections to put them down, the lab tests . . . it came to €15,000. Five grand a bird."

How did we miss that entry in the annual accounts?

Chapter 8 ~

WHY SELL TO GAA PEOPLE? PROFITING FROM BIG GAME TICKETS

S emple and the Hyde, the Park and the Athletic Grounds, and above them all, the Big House in Jones's Road. The GAA's stadium infrastructure is a trump card in the—usually—good-humoured ribbing among sports fans of differing persuasions.

The fact that hurling and football are serviced by stadiums around the country ranging in quality from good to outstanding is a major achievement that the GAA is rightly proud of. So is the fact that every county has a stadium it can point to as its best venue, one that suits the pageantry of a county final or an inter-county league game when TV cameras cast an unsparing eye over the facilities.

The only problem? Well, it's clear that some of those stadiums may be just too big. All over Ireland there are stadiums which county board officials admit, off the record, they never expect to see filled in their lifetime.

"One thing I would say is that I'd feel now that we'd be far better off with about half a dozen stadiums with a capacity of 30,000 or more, with their facilities developed to a high level," says Páraic Duffy, a remarkable comment from the GAA's director-general. "Take Munster. Pairc Uí Chaoimh, Killarney, Limerick and Thurles, all with 40,000 capacity. In Connacht you have Hyde Park, Castlebar—around 30,000. And Pearse Stadium—that makes seven. Croke Park in Leinster, and other stadiums holding 20,000, the likes of Portlaoise and Tullamore. With infrastructure we have to look carefully at what we want to do. Once Casement and Pairc Uí Chaoimh are done then that's the end of the big phase of infrastructural development. The era of major infrastructural spending is over for now. We invest less in infrastructure now because clubs are investing less."

The step away from bricks and mortar is endorsed by former GAA president Christy Cooney. "I agree fully with that. Does it mean more funding for games development? I think it means we stay consistent and we maintain what we're putting into that, into games development, and we put other funds into the upkeep of grounds, into keeping up with health and safety requirements and so on."

This is the crux: do you spend money on better sightlines and a shiny new roof for the stand or do you put more coaches on the ground? Cooney has no doubt about the future of facilities development—the doubts are reserved for the past. "Páraic is right. Outside Pairc Uí Chaoimh and Casement Park the big developments will now be limited. I don't think the money is there for it, and I also think we don't have a need for it. We probably have enough stadiums to manage our affairs.

"Going back ten or 15 years, would we have developed to the extent we did? Maybe we wouldn't, but the money was there. We got lottery grants; money was easily accessible in the financial world, money that's not there now, so you have to cut your cloth. The infrastructure committee has done huge work in recent years on standards and on how we spend money.

"Where I see the money going into are centres of excellence, for youth, which mixes the two, of course, infrastructure and youth, or games development. And that's hugely important, because the day we ignore what happens at school or club level, that'll kill the Association; it means you won't have the talent coming through."

Cooney concedes that the development of stadiums could have been approached differently. "We could have looked at our infrastructural plan for the development of our major stadiums ten or 15 years ago, and when there was plenty of money around we might have looked more closely at centres of excellence. But it's easy to say that now, and with the former you could say the Celtic Tiger was only starting at the time, and I think we're better for that. Our governance is better; our structures are better. We learn from things we could have done better, maybe, and in ten years' time people might be saying to me, 'Christy, you could have looked at this closer' or whatever. Fair enough.

"But overall I think we've managed our affairs very well. We're in a very good space. Do we have too many stadiums? Maybe, but that's a difficult one for counties, because every county wants a good venue for its big club games and so on, so you could be critical, but you have to balance that by looking at the overall."

That's a key point: you couldn't say to county x that they weren't to blow money on upgrading their main ground if county y next door had ploughed millions into its facilities. It's not a matter of snaffling inter-county games; it's a more parochial concern about staging your own county's big matches.

———

Which isn't to say an economist accepts that at face value, even one who's steeped in the GAA. John Considine, who's done academic research on attendances, takes an economist's detached view of stadiums and infrastructure, not to mention ticket prices.

"The GAA isn't a profit-making organisation and it therefore has a different model. That's why it wouldn't be out of the way for it to say, 'look, we could create more space in the calendar for the club player'—but there's also the commercial reality of paying for Croke Park. Re Croke Park, by the way, if you generate money, where do you use it? And do you need that (stadium) in the first place? I remember the late Con Murphy saying, when the clubhouse building boom was at its peak, what comes next? Floodlights were next, it turned out, then a new pitch, then an all-weather pitch. Do you do all of those? The ultimate goal, remember, is to fund all the other stuff, not to pay off backers."

Funding that other stuff still takes a considerable amount of money, though. Hence Considine's interest in ticket prices.

"Why sell tickets at a standard price for an All-Ireland final? Why doesn't the GAA set up its own hawking-type mechanism on the internet and sell off the tickets in phases? In addition, you don't have to fill the stadium. You could sell 80,000 tickets at €10 each, or 40,000 tickets at €30 each.

"I'd go further—look at the way they're given out. Tickets are allocated to the counties involved, and you have all this horse-trading. 'I'll give you one football for two hurling' and so on. Why not just sell to the highest bidder, even if those people aren't involved in the GAA, or sport at all? If you're prepared to pay €200 for an All-Ireland ticket, after all, and I'm only prepared to pay €20, why not sell it to you rather than to me? Now you might be a rugby supporter and none of your kids plays hurling, while I might be a member of the GAA with two kids playing hurling, but if I'm not prepared to put up the money I shouldn't get the ticket.

"The GAA doesn't see it like that, obviously. The ticket prices are set as a kind of reward for people. But you don't have to fill the stadium to maximise your money; that's my basic point. Fifty thousand people might pay a higher ticket price than 80,000 paying a lower price."

True, but there's an obvious weakness to this argument, one signalled by Considine in his first comments on the matter—the fact that the GAA doesn't generate cash to pay off investors: "There's a whole other aspect of this that feeds into stadium size. We build very big stadiums to get a big crowd, as many people as possible in to see a game. That's fair; it's what people want; but it's also because you have a different kind of organisation. If it were based on commercial realities it'd work differently—you'd have more music concerts in Croke Park to maximise revenue—but it's not based on commercial realities. It's a sporting organisation, maybe a cultural organisation, and there aren't many of those around."

But what about those very big stadiums for most of the year? Or somewhere like the Gaelic Grounds in Limerick, which is hardly filled once a year?

"Limerick might want a Munster final there, and that makes sense," says Considine. "But look at the rugby model: Leinster can play in the RDS—or Donnybrook, where they used to play—or the Aviva. They can move the game to suit the stadium. It's not about a spiritual home or anything like that. Now you could develop a range of stadiums in Munster, but it wouldn't be the same. Imagine playing a Munster football final in Waterford? How many people would go to that?"

So would it be better for counties to look at their 'second' stadiums in cases where there is more than one big ground available? To take the Leinster rugby model on board in Cork, for instance, would it make more sense to develop Pairc Uí Rinn, the second county ground, as a boutique stadium rather than ploughing millions into a huge redevelopment of the existing big stadium, Pairc Uí Chaoimh?

"It depends. If you were talking about non-live entertainment like the cinema, you get in for a lowish price but the soft drinks and popcorn are expensive. The GAA isn't like that. It doesn't sell you a cheap printer and charge you the sky for the cartridges. The GAA is about getting you to see the games, and you skimp on the service to do that. Maybe not in Croke Park, where you have good services, but in other stadiums. You could maximise in other areas, but the GAA wouldn't do that.

"If you really wanted to maximise revenue you'd sell the rights to the All-Ireland final to Sky Sports, but you couldn't see the GAA doing that. If you're playing an All-Ireland final you want to play in Croke Park because All-Ireland finals are played in Croke Park. It's not just a business model, but you are selling the fact that people are going to Croke Park."

The sense in which marketing a game in Croke Park isn't quite a matter of operating to a business model, and yet is, at the same time, is a neat crystallising of the book's central theme. Mind you, it's funny what Considine said about Sky Sports, as we shall see shortly.

Chapter 9 ～

CULTURAL STEREOTYPES: WHO BRINGS THEIR OWN SANDWICHES TO CROKE PARK?

Blaas and drisheen, coddle and oysters, the Ulster Fry.
Beamish and Murphy's in one southern county, large bottles in another. Clonmel Chardonnay—aka cider, or one brand thereof—the tipple of choice in yet another Munster county. We may live in a small country, but there's still a fair culinary range going from north to south. We're not even getting into the particular county well known for its reliance on ham sandwiches as one of the principal food groups.

As a consequence you'd imagine that the people who look after food in the Big House in Jones's Road would have a ready answer to this question: what county's supporters bring their own sandwiches to Croke Park?

Clearly we're tipping slightly into the realm of ethnic stereotyping here. Residents of the Munster county referenced above, for instance, while believed to collect sandwiches of a specific type at exit points from the region, tend to be sensitive about that tendency. Citizens hailing from a particular county in the province of Ulster are understood to be able to peel oranges in their pockets, for reasons best known to themselves, but they actively dislike attention being drawn to that fact.

Enough of this careless slander, however. What do the experts say? Can Croke Park bosses anticipate which supporters will turn up their noses at the food on-site in favour of their own native cuisine?

"Well, we crunch the numbers, but not to that level of specificity," says Peter McKenna. "After every game we look at the figures to find trends and so on, and many things can affect those numbers—the weather, the time of the game, who's playing, the first game or the second game.

"Generally speaking, the further people have travelled the more they'll use the facilities, and the more they'll spend. So if you have people coming from Mayo, Donegal, Cork, they'll spend more in the stadium because they've had long car journeys or rail journeys and they may not have had a chance for lunch along the way or whatever. They'll certainly spend more than Dublin people, because a lot of the latter, obviously, head home afterwards."

So ham sandwiches aren't taken off the menu when Tipperary are playing? Oranges don't get whisked out of the fruit bowls because staff anticipate Cavan supporters bringing their own? "No," says McKenna, before adding, with perfect timing, "Unfortunately."

PART THREE: PERSONNEL

Chapter 10 ～

THE NECESSITY OF THE COMMERCIAL AGENDA: THE GPA

Now that the Gaelic Players' Association (GPA) is officially part of the GAA, it can be difficult to recall the consternation that the player organisation caused only a few years ago. It was going to bring down the GAA, critics said; everything it stood for was contrary to the aims of the (larger) Association; it was elitist and exclusive, confrontational and brash; it was obsessed with money; and, of course, it favoured professionalism. Pay for play was the ultimate goal, which would tear the whole GAA apart. Mass hysteria, as Bill Murray said in *Ghostbusters*.

The GAA itself tried to strangle it early on by setting up an oddly similar body, the Player Advisory Group, which swapped initials around and resembled, in one writer's memorable phrase, the kind of works committee set up by management in companies nervous of union infiltration.

It turns out that the wilder criticism was wrong on most counts. The GAA survived the arrival of the GPA, which in turn has enunciated its commitment to the GAA's guiding principles. Formal recognition led to an end to the GPA's self-confessed reliance on "megaphone diplomacy". But the critics weren't wrong about everything. The GPA took a very keen interest in money early on in its existence, and with good reason. If it hadn't, then it wouldn't have survived

———

The GPA does a fine job in overturning your preconceptions from the very start. You call to the offices in Drumcondra, a key area in the Dublin GAA map, and when you head out with communications officer Seán Potts for coffee, the natural tendency is to turn into the doorway of Kennedy's, a traditional pub nearby. Potts, however, guides you up the road and around the corner into the preferred venue: a stylish crêperie.

Similarly, when you lob out the old charge of obsession with money and payment that used to be levelled at the GPA, instead of a pious rebuttal, Potts cheerfully concedes the point. The GPA had a commercial agenda, he says, because they had to.

First, though, the background.

"To understand the commercial agenda you have to examine the GPA historically, where it came from and what led to its creation," says Potts. "It was set up by players in the late 1990s in response to the rapidly changing environment in which they were playing; the growth in television coverage, the commercialisation of the GAA, the redevelopment of Croke Park. Players felt there was an imbalance there in terms of player welfare and wanted to influence their own changes. There was also an understanding among the players that they were now being exploited commercially, harnessed by the GAA in terms of television rights and sponsorship. There was a culture change within the GAA, particularly once you had names of sponsoring firms on the county jersey—the Rubicon was crossed then."

Interestingly, Potts can isolate the double edge to the "commercial agenda". He draws a subtle difference between what players were interested in, and what the GPA needed. "While the GAA's commercial agenda in part led to the growth of the GPA, it wouldn't be fair to say that the players just got together to see if there was something in it for them. They weren't in it for a quick buck. They felt something needed to change. Many counties did not have a good record in terms of the treatment of players, yet here was an organisation forging a new commercial reality, contracts worth millions created on the backs of players."

After the GPA was set up and moves began to improve welfare for players, the organisation's *raison d'être*, it also realised quickly that it needed to develop its own commercial agenda. As GAA members acknowledge elsewhere in this book, you can't run any organisation on optimism and a bright smile.

"Initial deals such as the Marlborough sponsorship of a group of players actually helped relax the rules on amateur status, allowing players to earn money from endorsing products," says Potts. "The GAA was probably moving this way anyway, but the GPA was a driving force. Of course the GPA's first tentative steps into the commercial world were greeted with suspicion by many within the GAA who viewed it as an organisation trying to railroad the GAA into professionalism."

"The whole debate around professionalism began in earnest following the creation of the GPA, but it was interesting that, at that juncture, the GAA began moving away from the ethical argument alone and started to include the monetary one. That is, that professionalism is not just wrong because amateurism is noble, but also it is wrong because it could not be sustained and thus would destroy the fabric of the GAA."

A cynic might point out that by switching the point of attack and addressing the sustainability of professionalism the GAA was putting itself in the position of Benjamin Franklin's famous virgin ("Neither a fortress nor a maidenhead will hold out long after they begin to parley"), but that kind of jab was a luxury the GPA could only afford in retrospect. It first had to make some money simply to exist, and early on that was a huge challenge. There were no guarantees the player organisation would survive its first year, for instance.

"The GPA had to drive on with its own commercial agenda otherwise it wouldn't have been able to survive," says Potts. "It was in the balance in the first 12 months whether it would last, particularly when the GAA set up its own rival players' committee. Initial sponsorship from Carphone Warehouse helped the players' body get off the ground, but the deal subsequently done with Club Energise was long term and underpinned the growth of the organisation. Besides the tensions over perceived agendas, the GPA was now in competition commercially with the GAA, and this commercial activity was regularly criticised. However, with players central, it served the purpose of focusing minds as well as securing the future of the GPA."

Here's another side to the GPA–GAA tension in the early years, of course, and one few people picked up on. There was then—and certainly is now, given the recession—a finite number of firms interested in GAA-oriented sponsorship and endorsement deals, and the success of Guinness and Bank of Ireland in sponsoring the hurling and Gaelic football championships respectively was as much a hindrance to the GAA as a help. It meant there were fewer blue-chip events and competitions the organisation as a whole could offer to potential sponsors. On the other hand its rival for commercial opportunities could offer businesses some of the most recognisable people in the entire country.

Despite the undoubted turbulence of those years, though, trust started to build gradually between the GAA and the GPA.

"I suppose when the GAA saw we weren't going away, that we were continuing to strengthen, pragmatism started to guide relations and several years before the GPA was finally recognised officially, the GPA was acknowledged as the *de facto* players' representative body," says Potts.

Still, even with peace on the horizon there was one last step to take, says Potts. Official acknowledgment wasn't just a matter of being welcomed to the party; it was a breakthrough in funding as well. If the GPA was going to function properly as a player welfare organisation, then it'd need more revenue.

"That *de facto* recognition was a big step forward, but it was the commercial 'agenda' that finally saw the GPA over the line. Formal recognition meant a deal on funding so that the GPA could implement its long-time ambition to implement a Player Development Programme.

"But when a deal couldn't be struck, the GPA used a commercial 'stick': players were withdrawn from broadcast interviews during one day in the championship. Some people called that action tokenistic at the time, but it was far from it. It was a shot across the bows of the sponsors—that was their space and the player was central to it.

"But we pointed out that as amateurs they weren't contractually obliged to do anything in that regard and they needed to take stock of that. The commercial aspect has been central to the GPA: we had to make money to survive, but that other awareness has developed as well."

————

What about the other great fear expressed by the GAA, professionalism, the shadow which replaced communism as a nightmare of (sporting) godlessness in the innocent land of happy amateur sport? What about the GPA inciting its members to take up the cudgels for pay for play?

In fairness, the player organisation could hardly be more unequivocal about professionalism for its members.

"Professionalism is not on the agenda," says Potts. "It never was and hasn't really been discussed since those early days of the GPA when it formed part of the regular debate about player power. It crops up with individuals, and it popped up during the managerial payment controversy because we were clear that we felt managers should be paid—that it should be formalised because it was an embarrassment to the Association.

"We were accused of driving the professional agenda—'the players will be paid next'—that kind of thing. It's simply not feasible. Dónal Óg Cusack's rationale has been criticised because it meant analysing the impact of professionalism, but he was clear when he said that the GPA would not be serving its members properly by advocating professionalism. Besides destroying the county game as it is, the lack of funds to tend to player development would ultimately be detrimental to the player. If you were addressing a roomful of GPA members you'd have to tell them that 75 per cent of them wouldn't be playing. You'd have to ask them if that's what they'd want."

Potts offers a neat summary of the double bind the GPA would find itself in with professionalism: "The GAA's amateur ethos is now enshrined in the GAA's constitution. The idle talk about secret, long-term agendas is nonsense. The bottom line is that there'd be no money for player development if the GAA went professional, so that would hardly fit with an organisation working for player welfare."

By the same token, though, the GPA does focus on the inter-county player (it's a not-so-secret, not-so-long-term agenda). The organisation's been criticised for ignoring the ordinary club player— or the ordinary club, come to that. Rather than deny that, though, Potts says there's a focus on the inter-county player for one simple reason: they're the people who generate the money that helps the non-elite player.

"We've been accused of being elitist, of driving a wedge between the county and the club game," he says. "The reality is that there is a natural divide between the different tiers and that has nothing to do with the GPA. We didn't create that division, but there's an elite level in the sport. That exists in all sports, and you have to have that.

"Our current view regarding commercialism is that we must continue to make the games as viable as possible, and the elite level has to be an attractive package. The players' profiles must be developed such as putting players' names on the backs of jerseys, promoting them locally and nationally. Driving the commercial agenda with the player playing a central part might seem somewhat self-serving on our part, but we would have genuine concerns about the future of the GAA and the county game, and we believe that ensuring the commercial health of the games is critical. And I'm not being too defensive about that.

"We've had critics saying we are damaging the GAA by prioritising county players and their development, by campaigning for government funding, but these critics are missing the point. By assisting with the development of the county player, supporting his commitment to the game, we can make a real difference."

Potts can even throw in an uncomfortable comparison or two: "When we were battling for government funding for players, some critics accused us of pushing the GAA the way of other one-time bastions of the country such as the Church or Fianna Fáil and it is an analogy I've since turned on its head. One of the reasons traditionally strong organisations can fade is a failure to change, to adapt, to plan. They say you're never as vulnerable as when things are going well, and while the GAA has had very good leaders in the last 25 years, it needs to continue to be bold and imaginative. Competition with other sports for hearts and minds continues to intensify. Look at the phenomenal growth in the popularity of rugby, the success of its marketing."

Fair enough, but what's the direct link between the top county player and funding for small rural clubs? If you're trying to scramble enough money together to buy jerseys for the U14s and you don't have a marketable county player in your club, what good is the GPA's commercial drive to you?

"Seventy-five to 80 per cent of the GAA's entire revenue is generated by the inter-county game," says Potts. "A very similar proportion of the GAA's entire revenue is recycled to the grass roots in all its forms through provincial councils and so on. It's a very relevant equation for us because it's the perfect response to people saying we're disregarding clubs and so on. We're not, and this is why. We're looking for a small slice of that funding to put in development programmes for county players—to sustain that inter-county game and the resulting revenue. And the reality is that although the GAA has funded the programme for five years our ambition for the services and their impact on the lives of players would outstrip that.

"Our long-term strategy would be to double the level of funding, but we're conscious that the ability of the GAA to fund us is limited and establishing new lucrative joint commercial ventures will be essential. And through our own fundraising we're trying to attract substantial benefactors to support our work. The relationship between the county game and the wider GAA is symbiotic, but we believe that a thriving inter-county scene will help sustain a healthy GAA. And the players are central to that success."

Chapter 11 ～

WHAT AN OLD GUINNESS AD TELLS YOU ABOUT GAA PLAYERS

You remember the Guinness television ad. A hurler is upended on a muddy pitch as a championship game comes to an end, and he stands over the free that could win the game. The defenders lining the goal turn into Lord-of-the-Rings-type orcs, the sliotar is transformed into a weight no one could lift, and the free-taker's mind drifts off to the debauchery of the celebrations if he scores (all of this with nary a helmet or face mask in sight, too).

There was a minor kerfuffle when it turned out afterwards that the actor who took the starring role in the advertisement was English, but it probably tells you how far players—and the GPA—have come that such a situation now would be practically unthinkable.

"TV coverage and player profile is essential to help market the games," says Seán Potts.

"That's what other sports do and I think with fears about professionalism allayed, the GAA can really grasp the nettle here. Ten years ago Croke Park was probably fearful of embracing players as their central marketing tool—actors were used in some of the early television adverts. But with a healthy partnership now in place, I believe we can really drive on and market the games at a different level. It is a little disappointing that the centrality of the county player isn't articulated more often.

"To be fair it is recognised in the Agreement between the GPA and the GAA, but the county player's contribution to the commercial success of the GAA needs to be promoted more. The redistribution of GAA revenue to the clubs is always highlighted in the GAA's annual reports, but not how that revenue is generated in the first place. It may be accepted, but there's no harm in highlighting it."

Particularly when it comes to what players put into inter-county careers—Potts says the commitment shown by those players is recognised by the general public, however. "During the grants for players campaign I think—despite the vocal opposition—there was a silent majority of people who supported it," he says. "People who felt players deserved a small reward, or deserved to be recognised by the State for what they contributed. I suppose that reflected a certain awareness of the cost to a player of playing at inter-county level. However, there's such a disparity between the levels it's difficult to establish the exact cost. One aspect that is noticeable is that county players are staying in college longer because it suits them, now that the economy has changed."

Potts is correct. You notice that more and more when you pick up match programmes—players in their mid-twenties listing a third-level institution rather than a full-time job as their nine to five commitment.

Is it just me, though, or does it seem that a high proportion of the players in work are teachers? If so, that leads to a rather leading question: if devoting yourself to an inter-county career is such a huge commitment, do you need a particular type of job to succeed at that level?

———

Dessie Farrell, GPA chief executive officer, mulls it over. He ponders the difference in demands on players first of all, and how inter-county commitments affect them. "That's disparate. If you're a player whose work involves night duty, weekend work, shift work, overtime, then playing will impact on your pocket because that's work you can't do. If you're self-employed it affects you.

"If you're in a profession then it'll affect you because if you're an accountant or a lawyer in a busy firm everyone else is trying to get ahead, meeting clients, impressing the boss—and you're off doing your own thing. Yes, teaching is the big one now because it seems to be tailored to the inter-county career and players are making a decision to go into teaching for the sake of their inter-county career, a job that helps them to do their best on the field."

There are obvious advantages to teaching if you're an elite GAA player, but Farrell points out that there are drawbacks which a young hurler or footballer doesn't always consider when making a career choice in his late teens or early twenties.

"And that's fine. It's a personal choice, but I'm not convinced players are making that decision and taking the bigger picture into account. It's a very narrow-minded focus to have at that particular time and while it might be beneficial for the inter-county career to be off for the summer and to finish early in the afternoon—and there's nothing wrong with a teaching career—long term it does place restrictions on a player's earning potential, while moving up the ladder can be quite difficult."

"There are a lot of careers players can't consider," says Potts, "because to all intents and purposes they can't pursue those for ten years. They couldn't work as journalists, for instance." (And a good thing, too, for all concerned.)

"Teaching is relevant because we seem to have more teachers than anything else," says Farrell. "But sports science is what they're going into now, though a lot of lads are moving into teaching from sports science as well. Teaching is a great career. Obviously it is, but all these choices come with consequences, and in terms of maximising individuals' potential, a lot of players could have very lucrative careers in other areas. But teaching is the decision they're making, and they're making it based on football and hurling rather than on other reasons."

This is where a player welfare organisation comes in, of course. The GPA places great store on its careers advice, and Potts argues the case for early intervention when players are considering their work options: "Emigration is still a threat. It's not a crisis at inter-county level but it is at club level, particularly on the western seaboard, and it's a threat to the viability of the game if high-profile players emigrate.

"It's about getting to the players early—they're making medium and short-term decisions based on their football and hurling. They're thinking 'at least I'm doing something', but 'something' isn't a long-term option. Meeting them one to one, getting to them early to see their potential, to steer them in the right direction and to support them then—all of that is more relevant now than when the economy was thriving and choices were plentiful.

"So many of our players would be tradesmen and obviously that work is largely gone. There is a large cohort of players which needs to be retrained, but committing to full-time education mightn't be something they want to do—they may be working part-time, never mind their inter-county commitment.

"But certainly the lack of time to develop careers affects players. Before they know it they're 26, 27, and their peers have come out of college and possibly had further training in their careers compared to inter-county players. It's a challenge for us and we probably won't know for another six, seven years, until lads have gone through this process, how effective the programme has been as a positive intervention."

The GPA wants to go even further and formalise the introduction of players to the elite level, says Farrell: "Something we'd aspire to would be putting in place a certificate, an induction programme for players: that to become an inter-county player they must go through this process where we can get at them, to use that phrase."

Of course, it's not all bad news for your career, being an inter-county player. Any number of former hurlers and footballers around the country can attest to the doors that sporting fame opens; almost every town and village in Ireland has a sign on its main street which carries a name familiar to GAA fans—pubs, insurance agencies, financial consultants, shops of all sizes.

It's interesting, though, that Dessie Farrell links player profile to the championship structure. As he puts it, recognition isn't just a matter of having customers who know your name before you introduce yourself.

"Recognition is a much wider subject. What feeds into that is how the GAA does its business, the championship structure—can we have more high-profile games, can we create more superstars, and so on. There are maybe 20 well-known players, yet we have a membership of 2,300 players. That comes home to us when companies or charities get on to us looking for a player: it's always the same names they want, which reflects how the games and the championship are structured. That's an issue the GAA has to grapple with, and obviously we have a role we can play in that, putting across our perspective. But in terms of the profile of the games, we need to look at broadening the shop window and having competitions that generate that level of appeal."

There are a lot of transferable work skills among inter-county players, says Potts: "Commitment, drive, discipline—and there's an emotional connection to inter-county players which is a help to players in business. Even knowing who an inter-county player is if he's coming to work in your house, there's a connection. But it's something we need to work on.

"For instance, we did a deal with PWC and while we were setting up the partnership we realised there were members of their team who didn't know who (Dublin player) Cian O'Sullivan was, though he was an employee of theirs and a recent All-Ireland medal winner. He now has an ambassadorial role there since the partnership was established, but his profile should have preceded that."

———

Recognition has a particular resonance within the GPA, associated as it is with the organisation's relationship with the GAA—and subsequent funding by the larger body. Having the GAA as an economic benefactor hands critics a handy entry on the charge sheet when it comes to the GPA's independence, though. Now that they're inside the tent, and all that . . .

"We hear that—'ah, ye're very quiet now'," says Potts. "But the reality is we can operate far more effectively behind the scenes as an officially recognised body. When there's a problem we go directly to Croke Park because we have a direct line now and our outcomes are far more positive than engaging in public spats. It mightn't always suit the media, but that's the reality of a working relationship."

It's certainly a different approach, if you can remember the era of veiled—and not-so-veiled—threats to withdraw players from media duties and so on. Potts adds that the GPA's occasional silence on live issues can be misleading.

"There was a time we used megaphone diplomacy because it was the only way we could make our point and I suppose it's a legacy issue for us. So you'll have an ill-informed commentator pointing out that the GPA's silence on a particular matter was 'deafening' when the reality is we are all over the same issue behind the scenes. We try to achieve good outcomes for players that way and we've been more effective since recognition than we were beforehand.

"Now it mightn't seem like that because we're not making noise. It can appear to people that making noise solves problems, but it doesn't. A lot of the time it's just making noise. If there's an issue with a player and he doesn't want us to say anything or it's more prudent not to comment then we won't, and there's silence."

The communications officer gives the fixture headaches that occur at club level as an obvious example of an ongoing issue the GPA is trying to address quietly. Again, it feeds back to Dessie Farrell's earlier point about the importance of the structure of the inter-county championship.

"One point about the relationship between the inter-county and the club games is that that relationship can be exacerbated by fixture issues within individual counties. And there's an obvious problem for the clubs in that they clearly want their county players for big games and they can't have them for long periods and so on. A solution to that will be found eventually. We're looking at different models for the alternative inter-county championship structures to promote a proper debate in this area and the GAA has made great strides in improving the club schedule already, so I suspect a solution will be found in the medium term.

"Players should be able to play with their clubs, but training regularly with clubs during the county season is a different matter. The GPA isn't against clubs—our players are club players. They started and will finish with their clubs. However, failure to look at the bigger picture, the shop window, would be catastrophic for the GAA and you simply can't have everything.

"We have a herd of sacred cows in the GAA. No one wants to make the really hard call to streamline competitions, so we have constant tension and squabbles between club, county, college, U21s etc., but the club is the natural unit of the GAA and county players are acutely aware of that. Dessie Farrell's last five years of football after retiring from Dublin were with his club and he was as committed to that as he was when he wore his county jersey. That's the way of things."

Farrell himself finesses the 'funded silence' criticism a little more by setting it in a global context. In other sports the funding relationship between governing body and player representative group is exactly the same, he says: "There'll always be a job of work there as far as I'm concerned. For the vast majority it's a good move, but the odd time you'll hear 'ah the GPA aren't saying anything on this because they're funded' or whatever. There's always work to do there, but now we engage with the GAA in a meaningful way. It's more constructive, but going about your business that way means people aren't aware of what's going on behind the scenes. But that's no different to other player organisations around the world. The NFLPA is funded through the NFL, the owners and so on, and that's been the case since that body was founded.

"I don't believe that long term it poses an issue—matters will arise which might have to be played out in the public arena, matters which might offset that perception. But in the early days you're doing your best to keep everything on an even keel, to keep the working relationship a good one. We feel there's a good amount of pragmatism on both sides, a need, from the games point of view, to keep the inter-county window operating as well as possible.

"On our side we realise we need a good working relationship to be able to do what we need to do. There's an understanding there."

Mind you, the player chief doesn't rule out conflict in the future, either. "Some people comment in ignorance on what's going on and it's difficult to educate everyone on what's going on, but long term I don't think that's an issue. There'll be enough happening in the future to prove that we have teeth in what we're trying to achieve for our players."

––––

All of this leads to one question we're fond of asking GPA members of our acquaintance.

What would happen if another player representative body came on the scene, demanding its share of the funding cake?

Donal Óg Cusack likes remarking that one revolution is enough in any man's life, but how would yesterday's firebrands react to a new breed storming the barricades? Dessie Farrell accepts the question as valid, but points to apathy as the main obstacle to a Provisional GPA.

"Where that could happen is at club level, club players mobilising for issues they're concerned with," he says. "But there are two things to bear in mind.

"One, from the earliest days, when we were at our wits' end with keeping this thing going, the degree of apathy among players was always huge. For some of us this consumed our lives, getting the GPA up and running, and it always flabbergasted us to come across players who were totally ambivalent about the whole thing. We'd be saying 'this is important to you, to your career' but . . . That exists with professional player representative bodies as well, by the way. But the chances of a group of players stepping outside something that's been organised for them—that'd be amazing. I don't think that would happen.

"Having said that, when we get to the stage that players are coming to our AGM with issues, unhappy with how we're doing things, to contest positions—that's when you know you're starting to move on, that there's a new dynamic in the organisation. It's useful, but it also brings its own challenges, and at the moment players are happy to be led. Now we throw that back at them, 'Lads, it's your organisation.

There's not just a staff employed in an office in Drumcondra.' Getting lads involved, getting actively engaged, that's a challenge, but it has been getting better in the last few years."

"We're increasingly in touch with players on a more regular basis," says Potts. "One time it was more public communication, reacting to situations, but now we engage with players much more on the ground through our development officers and so on; so there are more potential leaders of the future coming through, hopefully."

Chapter 12

WHY THE GPA SEES ITSELF AS A BULWARK AGAINST PROFESSIONALISM

The GPA makes some pertinent points about professionalism and amateurism, but not maybe in the way you're expecting.

The way they put it, to have the latter survive, you've got to work hard at the former.

"We need a big picture approach because we need to run our games in a professional manner," says Dessie Farrell. "Just because we don't have a professional elite doesn't mean we can't do our business in a professional way."

So you're saying to keep the game amateur everyone needs to work as professionally as possible?

"Absolutely."

The thing is, the GPA points out—correctly—that there's more to professionalism in sport than the most obvious example across the Irish Sea, if only the GAA would look further afield.

———

A recurring theme when interviewing people for this book was the need to look beyond Britain when it comes to economic models for the GAA's development. There are lessons to be taken from the National Football League in America, for instance, and the National Collegiate Athletic Association, as well as the Australian Football League down under.

When you think of professional team sport, historically your mind drifts to top-flight soccer in England, but there are other options to consider if you're open-minded enough. The player organisation is certainly willing to look abroad.

The GPA has a seat on the board of EU Athletes, a federation of European player bodies—they're also trying to set up a world organisation of player bodies—and as a result they can see the reality of pro sport.

"I was at a meeting there and you find a lot of them have the same problems," says Farrell, "trying to engage with governing bodies on issues, to influence change, moving things in the right direction, generally.

"Around ten years ago the Australian Players' Association was instrumental in convincing the soccer governing body to restructure how competitions were organised. They didn't go far enough and some of the decisions made then have come back to haunt them in terms of the location of franchises, for instance. However, it's seen as a great success, and that dynamic is going to be really important. But generally, it's very interesting. There are abundant studies which show that plenty of pro sportsmen hover just above the poverty line.

"FIFPRO has published what they've called the Black Book about football in eastern Europe, outlining corruption, match-fixing and violence against players—game in absolute crisis. There are probably historical issues in some of those countries, but there are also other problems, such as what we've seen here in Ireland in terms of kids trying to make a go of professional sport and being left on the heap when they don't make it."

The examples of African soccer players being exploited by unscrupulous agents and clubs in eastern Europe may be extreme, but Farrell's point is very valid. For every successful pro sportsman there are dozens who don't make the grade, and their sports don't always make adequate provision for their lives as civilians. Elsewhere in this book Donal Óg Cusack explains that that's not a route the GPA is taking, but Farrell says it can be difficult to even raise the issue in GAA circles.

"We feel there's a reluctance to look at the wider picture because of this fear of going down the professional route," says Farrell. "But if the GAA thought about it, we had an EU Athletes conference two years ago and we brought the delegates to an All-Ireland final. They were amazed because when they go home they're fighting their home associations for salaries for their players, clubs are going bust, and the professionalism is sucking the money out of the sport.

"I think with a bit of confidence, a bit of tweaking, we could have something really special here. At one of these conferences I made a presentation on Gaelic games, and hurling in particular, and the Japanese baseball delegation went crazy for it. They were mad for more information on it."

"We did it with music. We exported it all over the world," adds Seán Potts. "The Chieftains went from a group of young musicians playing in pubs to Carnegie Hall within ten years, and I know it's different, it's a cultural, artistic thing, but we've never done that with Gaelic games, and there's an important cultural component there too."

That reluctance to drive an overseas connection—apart from the Compromise Rules maybe, of which more anon—is linked by Farrell to historical factors: "One of the bugbears we have is that as an Association we've been somewhat reluctant to develop an international dimension. I suppose historically we weren't a global power and we didn't conquer countries and impose our games on them. But we were able to export *Riverdance* all over the world. When we were working in the States we were trying to set up some opportunities there, and the Yanks love their sport on TV. You see an Aussie Rules highlights package on ESPN, and that results in revenue going back to the game in Australia.

"When you see that, you say to yourself, 'Why do you need to head to a pub at eight in the morning to watch an All-Ireland final?' It's ridiculous. Why don't we have a weekly highlights package on ESPN? In terms of trying to broaden our horizons and infiltrate other markets, we're missing a trick there."

Potts chimes in with an example of a chance lost: "I was disappointed when I travelled to San Francisco with the 2011 Hurling Allstars as I felt it was something of a missed opportunity for an overseas trip. I suppose it shows that the player still isn't central enough in terms of marketing the games. I find that frustrating. There should be a big marketing push to promote the Allstars exhibition games in the States, a marketing blitz to generate publicity and attract an attendance."

"You're dealing with the culture, a throwback to the 'this is unique and very special', and if there's change you've to avoid the professional route . . ." says Farrell. "I think the GAA has to be more confident in itself, that we can embrace change, positive change, and bring on board what's best from other areas. All of that isn't going to impact on the bottom line—keeping the games amateur. If you look at it, people had a warped view of professional sports, either American sports or the Premiership, with vast wages that were threatening the existence of the sport."

———

Professionalism exists in the GAA, of course. Farrell points to the necessity for top-quality administrators, for instance, and the consequent necessity to cast a wide net to recruit same. If conservatism restricts discussion on professionalism within the GAA, then that conservatism can often be visible in appointments within the organisation as well.

"Part of what's needed there is a greater business mentality on the part of the GAA, even at county board level," says Farrell. "Paying more administrators to deal with the minutiae of day-to-day operations so the commercial directors can look at the big picture."

"We've to be careful not to go the same way," adds Potts. "Your core activity is your core activity and you can't get side-tracked into fire-fighting on individual issues rather than, say, working on a blueprint for a new championship. You only have a certain amount of resources and I think in fairness the GAA, to a certain extent, spreads itself too thinly in that regard."

You can't just rely on volunteers. Farrell wants aggressive recruitment of top-quality staff by the GAA: "The quality of professionals attracted to full-time administrative positions within the GAA needs to be looked at, particularly at county board level. I think there's a move to have that happen, but I think the experience in certain areas in that regard left something to be desired."

"They're important for the future success of the Association, to foster innovative thinking at county board level," says Potts. "Overcoming the fear of change is a huge challenge. Just because we are voluntary and amateur should not be a hindrance to professional development and ambition. There are many not-for-profit organisations in Ireland, in the arts for example, who combine both strands very effectively.

"Look at clubs. They have their own problems getting people in to do voluntary work, but that's true of all organisations, sporting, cultural, everything. The difference is that the GAA thinks it's unique with that voluntary dynamic."

Potts makes a strong point when he identifies a strand of thinking in the GAA that it's somehow the only organisation in the country with people giving up their time for free. The importance of the voluntary sector within the GAA can't be overstated in terms of its importance to the GAA, but other organisations rely almost entirely on goodwill to keep them afloat.

On a related issue, though, the sometimes condescending references to the rank-and-file members of the GAA often don't take full cognisance of who those people are, and what they think. Farrell points out that the political context in which GAA decisions are taken doesn't always take into account the sophistication of GAA members.

"One (potential) conflict would be the conflict of the professional and the voluntary. That can be a barrier to driving things on, because I know a lot of decisions taken within the GAA are taken on the basis of 'how will this play out among the grass roots'. And to be honest, the reality is that the grass roots, the so-called silent majority of volunteers, are progressive. One of the reasons it's important to embrace change is the redevelopment of Lansdowne Road and the millions taken out of the GAA coffers.

"That's because of narrow-minded conservatism, that 'ok, we'll allow games to be played there while Lansdowne Road is redeveloped'. If a more courageous decision had been made, we'd be getting €5 or €6 million a year from soccer and rugby games. And that's just gone now. Gone."

———

There are plenty of examples of issues playing out with the grass roots in the GAA. Seán Potts nominates the ongoing struggles with restricting county training—which appeals to club members because it would free county players for club duty and would presumably save money on training costs.

"There are calls to turn back the clock and restrict training at county level because somehow it is stretching the boundaries of amateur sport," says Potts. "Instead of finding a progressive solution, one that continues to enable players to train and prepare to the highest level, some would rather impose restrictions in a conservative manner. And they won't work. Yes, we need a closed season and yes, we need to restrict the number of competitions young players play in, but we need to do these things in a progressive manner and bring people along in the process.

"Complaining about the cost of preparing county teams is particularly annoying. I mean, where are the funds generated in the first place? And if they are not properly prepared, will we continue to attract crowds, sponsors and broadcasters?"

Dessie Farrell points out an anomaly in the complaint: "The cost of preparing inter-county teams is expensive, but that figure usually includes development squads, minors and U21s. It's usually couched as though it's a problem created by senior inter-county competition. If you don't spend the money and prepare them properly, what's going to happen? Standards will drop, fellas will feck off and you'll lose the best talent. That'd be the death knell. You need to put money into preparing players to reach the standards they aspire to. That's what drives the success of the games.

"As for preparation, again there's this fear . . . fellas want to prepare well; they want to train hard. That's a personal choice, yes, but when they make that choice they should be supported and helped in other important parts of their lives. But then you encounter the nervousness. 'Where's this going to end up?' You can't change the championship because you'll be placing too many demands on players. Look at the road we're on . . ."

If it's a road, then surely there's a destination. As Seán Potts points out, though, that destination doesn't have to be the inevitable one everyone thinks of: "People often ask that question, 'where'll this end up', and I don't have an answer to that. But what's interesting is that the only answer people have is professionalism. You will have people writing for 30 years that professionalism is inevitable, just like they were writing it 20 years ago."

"The other point is that there's a difference now compared to 20 years ago," adds Farrell. "Sport wasn't all-encompassing then. When I was ten years old you wouldn't have played rugby—the opportunity just wasn't there. You wouldn't have known where to go to play the game.

"The commercial success of Australian Rules, how they generate so much money, is very interesting. Fair enough, there's more competition in terms of TV, but the way they're making money off mobile content and so on, they're miles ahead. It's not enough for the GAA to say 'we're unique and we're different to every other organisation'. We should all be clear about this. The top players aren't paid, but every other component of the model is the same as other sports organisations. There's a professional administration tier, very dependent on the commercial success of the organisation and a huge voluntary grass-roots element—like professional soccer and so on. The model is more or less the same, but the GAA should be looking outside the country for best practice.

"How are they constructing TV deals in Australia for the AFL, for instance? What is the NFL doing, or the NCAA in America? What can we learn from them? There's a reluctance to engage with or use what works well in other sports. That was reflected during the introduction of red and yellow cards into the GAA. 'We're taking that from soccer', that kind of thing."

The last word on the GPA, harbingers of professionalism in some eyes, belongs to Seán Potts: "Ironically, in the long term, we would see the GPA as a bulwark against professionalism. I suppose the potential for the Kerry Packer-type situation exists. But the Player Development Programme, if properly funded, represents a real opportunity to safeguard the future of the GAA as a thriving, voluntary organisation."

Now that they're inside the tent, they're staying there. Potts says they're looking at presenting a paper on restructuring the football championships. The difference nowadays is that that's the kind of initiative which the GAA will take seriously. "If we hadn't been recognised, who'd care? But now we can do it independently but also as a driver of change. It mightn't happen immediately, but it should be able to stimulate proper debate on the subject."

Stimulating debate? You can be sure of it. The difference is now the debate takes place within Croke Park, not via megaphones outside.

Chapter 13

CAN HURLING BECOME MORE POPULAR?

Historian Paul Rouse points out elsewhere in this book that one of Michael Cusack's objectives in founding the GAA was to gain control of Irish athletics, which were hugely popular in the late nineteenth century.

Obviously that was an aim that couldn't be put on the new organisation's prospectus, but a wish to revive the old Irish game of hurling was a stated objective. Though the game is very successful in some counties it doesn't enjoy the far more widespread popularity of Gaelic football. Could economics be a contributing factor?

On the morning of the day I met Paudie Butler, former national hurling director, I wandered into a local sports shop to look at hurleys for my three-year old. The nearest I saw to her size was an O'Connor stick for €22. The shop didn't have any hurling helmets, but checking the Mycro website brought up an array of headgear, from standard at €75 to customised models at €90. The Quick Touch and First Touch Go-Game sliotars were €5 each.

This was before you considered the price of shorts, football boots and so on. The difference between Gaelic football and hurling, though, is that apart from the football itself, you only need shorts and boots to play football. Hurling can be a very expensive game to play: surely that's been an obstacle to its popularity?

———

Paudie Butler agrees up to a point. In his time as national director of hurling he travelled to the four corners of the country, literally, and probably has a better grasp of people's actual attitudes to the game, as opposed to their politically correct on-the-record support, than anyone else in Ireland.

"It was (an obstacle) until recently. In the Celtic Tiger time, the availability of money meant hurling became more accessible to people. Clubs and schools could buy helmets, and technology—the shatter-proof hurley—has made it particularly accessible in weaker counties, counties where a mother might buy a hurley for a child but wouldn't replace it. Certainly the economics were a huge influence on the spread of hurling up to the time of the Celtic Tiger, but I think a lot of clubs and counties are well stocked now. Nearly every school in Ireland has helmets; almost every club can access them. The manufacturers have been very good."

Another potential difficulty is the technical challenge of the game for children: the obvious problem for kids is that their legs are stronger than their hands, so kicking a ball comes easier than manipulating a length of timber that comes up as far as their waists. Butler sees the appetite among them for the game, though, and the strength of their enthusiasm is mirrored by good primary school-level coaching.

"From travelling around the country, what I've found is that almost every child in the country wants to play hurling or camogie. They want that chance. The children aren't the problem, and TV has done wonders in that regard. We've done a lot of good work in coaching, particularly in primary schools on introducing children to hurling, which is more tied to the primary curriculum than it used to be. In terms of expertise and giving kids the right start, we have a lot of people doing the schools, and that's going very well, but we don't have the number in the clubs, and that's a problem.

"I see that up the country, where you may have half a dozen people in a county who are interested, but they become overworked and burn out. And if one of those key people gets sick or moves away, the thing can fall apart. They're not replaced automatically. There are positive developments. Hurling clubs are setting up teams to serve the clubs in several parishes in some counties, for instance, so if a player wants to play hurling, he has an outlet. It's something like the divisional teams in some counties."

Other pluses include the relative disappearance of blood injuries in hurling now ("a real positive, particularly for young parents; the helmet, the laws and the general approach to the sport means there are fewer injuries") and the infrastructural legacy of the boom. People can decry the attitudes of the era, but at least something tangible was left behind.

"That's something which could improve things a lot," says Butler, "the number of astroturf pitches, particularly on the western seaboard, when conditions can become impossible. You could have viable hurling leagues on those pitches at a time of the year when football isn't up and running—provided they're full length and lit, of course. You also have indoor centres where U10s can play without being affected by weather. And I think because of all of that it's a good time for hurling.

"Those are bonuses from the Celtic Tiger, and clubs benefit from using those facilities, particularly in the off-season, when skill and technique can be improved. Those facilities mean that no matter where you're from or what time of year it is, you can practise at match speed the whole time with a hurling wall or astroturf; however, with a heavy field, long grass and bad weather, that match speed won't come. Those are great developments since the Tiger, and they're there, and we have them now."

Ever the optimist, Butler can even see some sunlight peeking through the current economic storm clouds. Unemployment is not something anybody welcomes, but a GAA club can at least offer an outlet.

"One upside of the downturn is that we have help available, with people offering their time. A man has to do something with himself, and if he's unemployed, severe as that is, at least he can make a contribution at his club that helps. With the Tiger you had money—and that went into facilities—but no time, while now we don't have the money but people have the time."

———

One county which spent money well, he says, was Dublin. Their rise to top-four status in hurling is often traced to the 60 development officers the Dublin County Board employs, and Butler says that paid coaches make a difference. Amateur ethos or not, having bodies in the fields can only help.

"The great majority of Irish people are living now in urban areas, no matter where their parents came from," he says. "We have a tremendous rural model, but that doesn't transfer to the urban area. I could name 20 towns with 1,000 schoolchildren each—and only one club. We need more clubs for those kids, because it's not reasonable to expect one club to provide expertise and training for all of them.

"The Dublin plan, that's what I think the big cities need. Cork and Belfast aren't as big, but that template will work for them, a games development officer attached to clubs and schools. If he can get voluntary people involved, fine, but he's the constant presence. There's an affinity there and the kids see him as the face of the GAA. That's the GAA in its best form, aiding and attracting: giving, in other words.

"It's the nature of the GAA to give rather than take, and we don't want to be seen as taking. If we can assist the schools, in particular, it'd be invaluable. You now have huge urban schools which are probably unaware of the existence of the local club in a way that wasn't the case 15, 20 years ago, so you have to have a presence in those schools. I see no way other than having full-time people doing that job. In general, though we have better methods and a lot to offer, we don't want to be dependent on full-time people. We need them to be attached to the club. I think the Dublin model has worked. Every time I go to Dublin I see kids with hurleys, supervised or not."

Other urban areas have not fared so well. The larger towns and cities offer a captive audience which hasn't been targeted, though Butler is hopeful they can be helped.

"Cork city has only a couple of people, and the city needs at least a dozen coaches. If I had unlimited funds I'd focus on Cork. In a lot of places you have the tradition of hurling, but not the numbers—rural areas where the population isn't what it was. But you have the numbers in Cork and the tradition. That would be my first focus.

"Then Galway city and places like Tullamore, Kildare, Meath and Louth, because you have the population there as well. A couple of those counties are ready to take the step to the next level because they're close to Dublin. They know the model and top-class challenge games are available to them. It's funny, by the way, that there was a time the Dublin clubs came down to us (Tipperary) and Kilkenny for challenges and we'd hammer them, but now they come down and hammer us, and we're asking to come up and play them."

There are green shoots, he says. Not all the urban centres are wastelands.

"Limerick city is on the way back; Na Piarsaigh and Ardscoil Rís are showing that. The Cork schools are two steps back, while in Waterford you have Coláiste na nDéise and De La Salle. The united colleges team is offering a lot to many counties, and the Dublin use of that model is one of the keys to their success. That's not easy. You have kids being pulled in all directions, but the other side of that is to make it to the top level you must serve your apprenticeship."

The blossoming at secondary school level is no accident, but Butler is keen to see the good work continue once kids are out of sixth class: "What you're seeing are the fruits of a terrific primary school programme. We can't abandon them at secondary level, as they come in competent to play. You might have only two or three GAA-oriented teachers in a school of 40 teachers, and they're going to be overstretched."

Unpaid coaches like secondary teachers face their own challenges, of course. The disappearance of the Christian Brother, effectively, from schools may have removed a cohort of unpaid GAA coaches from circulation, but Butler doesn't look back on that era with rose-tinted glasses.

"There's no question times have changed. The absolute trust in everybody has gone, and a male coach who comes in now must prove himself in every way—that he's kind, gentle, has an understanding of the nature of children and, above all, that he can guarantee the safety of the children in his charge. To that end he must bring in people with him to manage the team, because the day of one person doing everything is over. You'd like to see one of those people with expertise and the others with an air of care for the children; if the latter are with an expert they'll learn to do things anyway.

"I don't think anyone hankers back to the past: the day of one person knowing everything and telling people what to do—the 'command and control' model—is gone. Any teacher or principal will tell you that. It's more healthy and vibrant now, and the old days of one voice, while it worked to some level, we saw the repercussions when the wrong people got into power, when they manipulated their way into the system."

———

As a coach with decades of experience behind him, Butler recognises the need for professional teachers of the game's skills, and the relative shortage of candidates for that role. But he doesn't just want technocrats in the middle of a field blowing a whistle; times have changed and a whole new approach is needed for kids of all ages.

"We need a cohort of people committed to coaching—and a cohort committed to managing, because it's becoming more and more clear that there are two roles, and that coaches may not manage and vice versa. There's a coach education system from foundation to level four, and that's more helpful than someone coming in off the street and getting a team, and failing—and feeling the failure is their fault. Coach education would show them that failure is part of the growth, and that we all fail and we learn from that—that failure is part of learning, that teams could fail for one hundred years and then fail again before they eventually succeed."

Again, though, the traditions of the game make their presence felt—and not in a helpful way. Butler has no time for the traditionalist view that only those from certain counties could possibly know anything about hurling. He says it turned people away from the game, pure and simple.

"That's done hurling a huge disservice. Eamonn Ryan was the first person to draw my attention to that, the disservice we were doing by making hurling elitist. We turned off good people who wanted to give their free time, people who'd pick up enough . . . I saw it happen up the country, people from Cork or Tipperary or Kilkenny being given teams just because of where they were from. These were people who had no interest in taking teams back in their own place!

"But that is changing. I see young lads from Kerry making it in Australian Rules, having played senior football for their county, or inter-county minors coming through as rugby internationals. So we shouldn't be elitist. And being elitist didn't do us any good with hurling. My driving force is that every child living in Ireland has the right to catch a hurley and play the game. Whatever they do afterwards is their choice, but at least as children they should have that opportunity."

The economics of getting started in hurling are a little easier if the lead shown by some clubs were to be followed nationwide. "With helmets, it's not an everyday expense," says Butler. "If a child likes hurling, they'll buy a helmet and they'll have it for four or five years at least. And a lot of clubs are buying back smaller helmets when kids grow out of them, which makes buying the next helmet a little cheaper. We have lighter sliotars and shorter hurleys.

"That was one thing we underestimated in terms of the damage it did, by the way, bigger and heavier hurleys for children. We didn't understand that that removed their enjoyment, and that was happening more in the traditional areas than anywhere else, and we didn't understand why until recently. A child saw daddy coming home with his hurley and wanted that hurley, naturally enough, but it was too big and heavy for them to use. Now you go into primary schools and if you give children small, light hurleys, within 20 minutes they'll be able to manipulate them, which is far better.

"Can we provide enough coaches for all the children in Ireland? Places like Mayo and Donegal, though far-flung as counties, have increased participation by 300 per cent, but when those kids come through will there be games for them? Will traditional football clubs become proper GAA clubs and deliver on all the games of the GAA? You could call that a political problem, but that's the big discipline that we're missing."

It's an old bugbear of Butler's, giving kids the chance to play the full range of GAA sports. ("For me the ultimate discipline would be if the chairman of a county board, or division or club, made all the games of the GAA available, to give every child the opportunity to play hurling, football, rounders and handball"), but he's too positive to grumble about the game. He even finishes with another twist on the economics of hurling: the fact that its greatest, both those on the sideline and the men in combat, are unpaid.

"As for Kilkenny dominating being good or bad for hurling . . . looking at soccer results across Europe this year, it was the same story—one or two clubs dominate in every country. You get waves like that, and people say 'if Barcelona win it's not good', but they also say 'if Barcelona win ten in a row that's not good', so we tend to have a negative outlook. Kilkenny are playing at a level like See The Stars, like Tipp did in the sixties, like Cork have done several times. Is it good or bad? When Tiger Woods was dominating golf they said it was good for golf, so why wouldn't this be good for hurling?

"Ultimately, when their dominance is over, it will be seen as good for hurling. In the thousand primary schools I've been to, the kids all want to hurl and I put that down to the total excellence that's visible on television. You have had an extraordinary manager develop, perhaps in ways he doesn't understand himself, with terrific coaching, to produce players of extraordinary high calibre of discipline, mentality, togetherness and calmness within themselves. It's a good replica for every youth in Ireland—there's no loud-mouthedness, no boasting, no trouble. There's no foolishness or arrogance in any form, and they're a counter-argument to the Tiger.

"I feel Brian Cody is as good a manager as exists in the world, and he's a volunteer. That's an extraordinary statement. Maybe we don't do a lot of talking about that, talking that we should do.

"The same goes for Jimmy Barry-Murphy, Liam Sheedy, all of these people. If we don't value what they do then we're destroyed as people. If we value money more than that . . . the GAA has a lot to offer in that sense."

Chapter 14 ～

THE COMMERCIAL PRESSURES ON REFEREES WHEN IT COMES TO LATE EQUALISERS . . .

I t came up earlier when Tom Ryan was talking about revenue and replays, and it remains one of the classic complaints about the GAA.

A big game, a big crowd, and big performances from both sides means that with a minute or two to go there's only a point in it. Even the commentators say on radio and television that neither side deserves to lose, and play drifts towards the end of the field defended by the side trying to hold out, trying to maintain that narrowest of leads.

At this stage everybody is looking at the referee in expectation of a free which will give the trailing side another day out, and for many years the official seemed to oblige; that free was awarded, which meant a replay, and another bumper gate for the GAA.

Granted, the formal announcement of time to be added on undercut the process a little, as it brought to an end legendary stories of seven, eight or nine minutes being played in order to manufacture, finally, a match-levelling free. But even in 2012, when referee Barry Kelly awarded Galway a late chance to level the All-Ireland senior hurling final against Kilkenny, there was a) a certain amount of 'told you so' being thrown around; and b) an instant totting up of the financial windfall the GAA would enjoy as a result of the replay.

It never came as a surprise when that whistle was blown back in the days of injury time being at the referee's discretion. The only novelty was the array of conspiracy theories aired when the spectators started heading for the exits afterwards. Within seconds of the end of the game someone usually posited an ostensibly well-known fact about the match official: he was known to be a guest of one of the participating counties every year at their county final, for instance, put up in a five-star hotel and treated like a king for the weekend.

No, said another voice who had it on very good authority that in his business the ref had to do a lot of work in the county which needed that equaliser: he couldn't expect a warm welcome from his clients there if he hadn't come through with that late free.

Nonsense, said an authoritative voice, braying that everybody knew that referees in the GAA were under orders to create draws whenever possible to ensure another huge payday for the Association.

And everyone listening nodded along in agreement as they made their silent plans for the replay.

———

Dickie Murphy is still missed by many hurling supporters. The Wexford man was the country's top hurling referee before hanging up his whistle—at inter-county level, anyway—and his smiling approach, leavened with a good deal of common sense, is often cited as the ideal template for any referee.

You put it to him that it's almost part of GAA culture that a close game angling towards a one-point margin with time almost up will almost always produce an equalising point, courtesy of the referee; that it's almost an unconscious reaction on the part of the offical, a decision he makes without being fully aware that he's doing so.

Murphy rejects the suggestion completely.

"You wouldn't be thinking that. You wouldn't be at it too long if that were the case," says the Wexford man. "It's perception, pure and simple. A game ends in a draw and people say, 'ah, he made a draw of it'. But I can tell you it's the last thing on a referee's mind. If the game goes that way and it's a draw, fair enough. But thinking about the possibility of a draw while the game is going on, that you'll be popular with the Munster Council or Leinster Council or whatever? Not a chance."

Murphy argues his case with persuasiveness, pointing out that the sensory overload of a provincial final or one of the final games in the All-Ireland series makes it unlikely that the financial windfall due from a draw would be at the forefront of any official's mind. "With everything that's going on in a big game, say an All-Ireland final—the noise, the sights, fellas ploughing into each other out on the field— you're only trying to get through the game, to make the right calls, not to make a mistake. You haven't time to think of anything else, to be honest. You're trying to keep up with the play; it's going from one end of the field to the other.

"Thinking about a draw? No."

———

Referees don't make a killing on the biggest days of the GAA calendar, by the way. An All-Ireland final may draw well over a million viewers on television, not to mention 82,000-plus pilgrims in Croke Park itself, but the standard remuneration applies for the man who throws in the ball. There's no bonus because you're the one facilitating one of the biggest days of the sporting year.

"No, it's the same as a normal inter-county game," says Murphy. "Same as a national league game—50 cent a mile and your meal allowance. You don't get a sponsored car or anything! It's the honour of doing it. An All-Ireland final, it's history. Minor, junior or senior, an All-Ireland final is something that any referee worth his salt would want to do. He wants to handle an All-Ireland final the same as a player wants to play in one."

The referee's income has been the subject of some official focus in recent times. The Revenue Commissioners served notice, for instance, that they intended to look into referees' expenses. Murphy can offer testimony from the other side of that equation, a witness statement that suggests Revenue might be as well off searching for undeclared riches somewhere else. "Yesterday I drove to Taghmon for a game," he says. "I was gone at three o'clock and back at ten to six. Your whole afternoon's gone as a result. My wife had no car because my young fella needed it, so she had to sort out a lift home from work, so that was a hassle for her, obviously. And for what? For €30."

Clearly that's not a huge amount of money, and Murphy points out that there's a self-regulating aspect to the reimbursement that a referee can earn. There are only so many games in the day that an official can handle, perhaps three on a weekend if all were played at the same venue; no more than two if there's any element of travel involved.

How much money can a referee actually earn to make it a profitable proposition as opposed to just breaking even?

"It's great to have a referee at games, particularly local games: it's good for standards," says Murphy. "You get involved because you're interested, because you want to be involved, but who's making money out of that? You're gone for two or three hours away from your family, travelling and so on. I know that the players are doing it and aren't getting a penny for it, which is fair enough, but I think it's a bit much for the Revenue to be coming after referees for a few bob like that."

Murphy also notes that if GAA referees are under the microscope now, then match officials in other sports are bound to be scrutinised eventually.

"I'm conscious that the way the country is gone that they have to look at everything, that they need to see where they can get money, but I think it's excessive. And if it happens in the GAA you can be sure it'll happen in soccer and rugby and other sports as well. Obviously you're not in it to make money—you'd want to be refereeing a couple of games every night of the week to do that—but people shouldn't be out of pocket for facilitating games either. I couldn't justify the trip I made to Taghmon for €13 a game or whatever was suggested."

As this book was going to print the *Irish Examiner* broke the story that Wexford referees were to be asked for their PPS numbers, though that related to the county board getting a lower rate of tax liability on officials' expenses if such information were volunteered. In any case, don't expect a rash of draws due to the decisions made by Dickie Murphy and his colleagues in the south-east.

Chapter 15 ❧

THE KERRY PACKER SCENARIO

*K*ieran turned off the engine of his Porsche Boxter and hopped out on to the footpath, pausing before he entered the Shelbourne to admire its sleek lines and blood-red colouring. The little perks of being Hurler of the Year, he thought, bounding up the steps and into the hotel.

As he passed through the lobby, the knot of teenage girls shrieked and surged forward as one, proffering autograph books and—if he wasn't very much mistaken—a couple of phone numbers. Kieran signed his name dutifully. No need to repeat that unfortunate incident when he'd brushed off that kid in the wheelchair outside Semple Stadium, he thought: pity he'd been papped just at the moment he'd kicked the little chap's foot.

Security personnel ushered the girls away and Kieran proceeded to the function room, where he was scheduled to do some press on a—what was it? He checked his diamond-encrusted Android, and the message was still there. Today's gig was pushing those luxury flats in Dubai, though with the economy in its current state, it looked like he and his team-mates would be the only ones who could afford them.

Just as he entered the room, his other Android—the one kept for sports-related issues—cheeped loudly. He'd been having some

*problems over his hurley sponsor, hopefully that had been . . . No, it
was one of his agents. The move he'd been dreaming of for so long had
come through.*

*Kieran punched the air before settling down in front of the display
photographs of the sandy dunes and blue skies of the Middle East. He'd
be playing for the All-Ireland champions next season, kitted out in the
red, white and blue of New York . . .*

———

A fantasy?

One of the GAA's proudest boasts is that the 30 men who draw
80,000 spectators to Croke Park on All-Ireland final day are amateurs
who don't get a penny for their efforts, a statement usually made as
an endorsement of the amateur ethos rather than as a criticism.

It's always a surprise to foreign visitors, who have never seen
hurling or Gaelic football until they land on these shores, to learn
that the players are amateurs, and in general the impression is given
that professionalism would be tantamount to dousing every GAA
premises in the country in petrol before setting it all off with a lit
match. The GAA: the Greatest Amateur (sports) Association in the
world.

Certainly the financial implications of professional county teams
within the GAA are sobering enough to stop any accountant in his
tracks. Take the most basic breakdown of the 32 counties competing
for the All-Ireland football championship, with each carrying a squad
of 26 players. If those players were professional—signed to guaranteed-
wage per annum contracts—then the cost would be staggering.

If you start with the average industrial wage as a baseline, that
would mean €37,500 multiplied by 26 at the low end of the scale.
This wouldn't take account of professional support staff—masseurs,
physios, doctors—but we can cheat a bit there because county boards
already pay for professional medical and rehab care anyway. Still, it
leaves counties with a basic wage bill of €975,000 each. The word
'basic' is necessary because presumably the superstars on each team
would command higher salaries, but it'll do as a starting point.

That cost would be doubled in the case of dual counties, of course. We'll exclude those involved in the lower tiers of inter-county hurling and take only counties which compete at the highest hurling level for the Liam MacCarthy Cup: that would leave a dozen or so counties facing a wage bill of €1,950,000.

Clearly for smaller counties in particular that figure looks unsustainable. It's a commonplace of close-season GAA reporting to feature horror stories from counties which have to deal with the consequences of an unexpected run in the championship; after the happiness subsides the county board treasurer is left to tot up the bill, and the headline 'County Board faces 300k bill' was a hardy annual even in the unprecedented boom of a few years past, let alone the straitened circumstances of the present.

There's another consideration involved as well: the culture of the GAA we mentioned above. It's one of voluntary effort at club level, wherein the man lining the field at the smallest club in a county shares in the glory of that county's biggest day in Croke Park. A lot of hot air is exhaled about the volunteer ethos within the GAA, but it exists and is the biggest asset the Association—and any other sporting body—relies upon. However, neither money nor tradition is the reason the GAA is likely to remain amateur. It's because professionalism wouldn't be good for the players.

———

The notion of what's appropriate for professional sportsmen may appear to be an odd angle to take on this subject, but that may owe more to our most immediate experience of professional sport. Certainly Irish attitudes to professionalism in team sport owe a lot to English soccer: for a century Irish sports fans have followed the top English teams through their ups and downs in the leagues across the water, and for the last decade or two they've followed the top English players through tales of off-field excess after excess, so it's not surprising we take our model of a pro from that environment.

Often it's not a pretty one, with the players coming across as immature and unpleasant personally, to put it mildly, not to mention being immeasurably remote from their followers due to the large sums they earn. Those vast earnings are only possible in a large economy like Britain's, however, with a population almost 15 times the size of Ireland's. Still, there are other professional team sports which Irish sports fans can see at closer quarters.

Rugby dropped its amateur status a decade and a half ago and most of the top Irish players play for the four provinces at home rather than in the English Premiership, which was where a lot of them went at the dawn of the professional era. That still makes only four fully professional squads in Ireland, perhaps 120 players making a living from the sport. They're not paid at the same rate as professional soccer players, but top rugby players in Ireland can make €300,000–400,000 per year, though fringe squad members may only earn one-tenth of those amounts.

The economics of professional rugby means that even at the top end rugby players don't make the colossal amounts that top soccer players earn, which means that when they retire they'll have to get a job. That brings us back to what's appropriate to a person as a professional sportsman.

Getting a job in the real world after life as a professional rugby player isn't that easy. Quite apart from the recession, there are only so many coaching and media jobs to go around, and a player who hangs up his boots in his early thirties can find himself woefully unprepared for life beyond the playing field.

The kind of reality encountered by sports heroes when the cheering fades has coloured the thinking of one influential GAA personality when it came to professionalism. Donal Óg Cusack is famous for many things: for being the Cork hurling keeper, for his All-Star awards and All-Ireland medals, for being the first GAA star to out himself as gay, for leading his Cork team-mates through a variety of strikes with the Cork County Board and for his involvement with the Gaelic Players' Association. In the latter capacity he's often sat down to strategise about the future direction of the player movement with his GPA colleagues; with those colleagues he's discussed the future of the Association with the GAA's top brass and the role players would have in that future.

"When we discussed all of this, of course all the different scenarios were looked at by the different stakeholders, and the different impacts those would have," says Cusack. "That included professionalism, among other issues.

"Speaking personally, one issue which was critical was this: if it could be sustained, how would it serve the individual concerned? My feeling on that—our feeling on that—was that you wouldn't be serving the individual very well if you brought him into that environment because, with all due respect to professional sports people, everyone knows that that environment isn't always good life training. Putting a GAA player in that environment could create false expectations—until he's injured or drops out of the scene."

Typical of Cusack, he flips the scenario around. We see professionalism as a privilege, while he perceives the responsibilities that come with being a paid sportsman.

"A big challenge for the GAA would be to define what exactly an inter-county player is—what's expected from him? Does he know what he's getting himself into when, at the age of 18 or whatever, he's invited on to a senior panel and he becomes an inter-county player?

"That's a very interesting question for me, for the GAA and for the player movement within the GAA, and it ties into professionalism because it speaks to the expectations and demands that are placed on an inter-county player. If you asked 20 different inter-county players 'what exactly is an inter-county player', you'd get 20 different answers. When a player joins an inter-county panel a balance needs to be struck between his rights and his responsibilities, but those responsibilities aren't defined in any way, except according to massively wide parameters, so it's unfair of the Association to try to get that player to behave in a particular way.

"My own view there is that we may be selling the 'new' inter-county player a vision of something that isn't true—a way of life—and that they don't understand. Playing inter-county hurling or football is an enriching experience. Of course it is. But I feel that we should define what an inter-county player is in a better way. There are all sorts of challenges for players—talking to the media and having one of your comments picked up as 'criticism' of an opponent. Walking down the town after a game and getting abused by drunken supporters. I don't know if professionalism, however you define it, would help with those challenges."

———

The GAA has plenty of challenges when it comes to amateurism, of course. Close observers of the GAA can point to contradictions and hypocrisies everywhere in hurling and Gaelic football when it comes to money.

Inter-county players are employed in many county boards as games promotions officers, which means they spend their working days with a hurley in their hands or a ball at their feet, for instance. It's all above board, but surely those players have a competitive advantage over opponents spending their work days in an office or on a building site.

On a more philosophical level, the inter-county grant scheme introduced in 2008 for players carried a little-noticed item in the fine print about recipients' tax compliance being their own affair and not the GAA's, inviting the term 'independent contractors' to be applied to individual players when it comes to the hurling and football championships.

Looking to the sidelines, there is also the vexed question of paid managers, a long-running issue which the GAA has wrestled with openly but never fully addressed. Managers are entitled to legitimate expenses, but the grapevine within the GAA fairly crackles with tales of vast sums finding their way into the bank accounts of various glamorous coaches.

If the players, as stakeholders within the GAA, are broadly happy not to be paid professionals for whatever reason—economic or cultural—there seems little chance of pay-for-play becoming a reality, as Cusack says. Yet there's an obvious avenue for professionalism. It means you just have to broaden your horizons. Literally.

———

The lift to Shannon for a flight west has long been an option for talented inter-county stars following an early-summer exit from the championship, with various sweeteners extended for the trip across, from jobs to money. Those sweeteners come courtesy of the powerful backers of certain clubs in the big American cities; in the eighties in particular it was common for such GAA teams to be packed with inter-county stars on lucrative summer stays. It would be ironic if a situation in a foreign field to which the GAA turned a blind eye for many years—out of sight, out of mind—were to become the spark for professionalism within the Association at home.

But one man doesn't rule that out.

"The will isn't there for professionalism in the GAA," says Cusack. "When I say that, it's not there among the stakeholders—the supporters, the Association and the players. That's the fundamental thing.

"Is it possible? What would happen if Sky TV felt 'here's an unbelievable product; we're looking for a new product; how can we make this happen?' If that were to happen then you'd be coming close to making it possible. I'm biased, but I think hurling is a more unique sport than Gaelic football and would be a unique product for a TV company."

Parallels? Some readers may not remember events such as Kerry Packer's Flying Circus back in the late seventies, when Packer, an Australian media mogul, ran a parallel cricket competition in defiance of the international cricket establishment. He signed up then-prominent players for his World Series Cricket competition in an attempt to secure broadcasting rights for cricket in his homeland, and there was a lengthy stand-off between a conservative establishment and the brash newcomer, but eventually Packer pressed on and enjoyed three seasons of success with his 'Flying Circus', as a hostile English press dubbed his competition.

Packer and his adversaries kissed and made up, but there was little doubt about who had won the battle of wills. Packer changed cricket for ever and showed that even the most apparently conservative sport can change.

So if there were a Kerry Packer type who decided to break out and set up his own empire when it came to hurling? Cusack runs with the idea.

"Okay—what would happen if, say, someone took over an inter-county team outside Ireland, like London or New York, and made that team professional? What would happen if he brought the best hurlers out and gave them contracts? Specifically, what would teams back in Ireland have to do to measure up to that professional team? And what would happen to the GAA then? Would they find a way to get rid of them or would that team have to be matched? That all comes back to will, and the will to do it—or not to, as the case may be."

And if those things came to pass, what then? Those with an apocalyptic turn of mind would foresee the end of the GAA as we know it. Cusack isn't so sure.

"I think the changeover would be unbelievably difficult—really, unbelievably difficult—because there would be elements strongly against it, but after ten or 15 years it would just be treated as the norm. Look how fast amateurism toppled in rugby, after all. Has it affected the volunteer ethos in rugby? I doubt that, and it became normal very quickly.

"This isn't a cheap shot at anybody, but the president of the Association (then Christy Cooney) was paid a lot of money. I believe the president of the GAA should be paid well, because in general to get good people you must pay well, but while that doesn't add up for me, it comes back to the point I made earlier—the GAA can pay that money and accommodate managers being paid, for instance, because the will is there for that."

The will doesn't exist for professionalism among GAA players, though. Not now. That's clear. But that doesn't mean it'll never exist.

PART FOUR:
COMMERCIAL PARTNERS

Chapter 16 ∿

SUPER SUNDAY ON THE WAY:
MEDIA RIGHTS I

The tension sometimes sours into conflict. Not often, but occasionally. In his 2012 annual report GAA director-general Páraic Duffy hit out at media coverage of GAA games, with a particular emphasis on TV.

RTÉ was the target, and Duffy was soon supported by former GAA president Seán Kelly. ("I would feel the GAA have a strong case to get more television coverage for Gaelic games," Kelly told John Fogarty of the *Irish Examiner*. "I certainly agree with Páraic Duffy in the point that he's making because number one, they're the national broadcaster, and number two, Gaelic games are by far the most popular games right throughout the country as seen by participation and support. If they're reflecting where their money is coming from, that would suggest the GAA certainly has a strong case for more coverage.")

In discussing GAA revenue generally for this book, Duffy focused on media rights at one point—with some interesting revelations about the future for the Association.

———

First and foremost, Duffy is aware that the usual constraints experienced elsewhere in the GAA don't really impinge on the organisation's headquarters. He knows that even as county boards and clubs struggle for funding and have to find ever more imaginative ways to find revenue streams, it's the opposite situation for Croke Park: in large measure the money comes in anyway.

"We'd be conscious in Croke Park that we're lucky when it comes to the economics of the GAA," said Duffy. "If it's gate receipts, TV rights, sponsorship—the big money comes into Croke Park, and in running the operation we would never run at a loss. Nor should we. But whatever we take in, that's the basis of what we give out. That's the starting point when it comes to the target of redistributing 80 per cent of what we take in.

"For us the first thing is we try to generate as much as we can within certain parameters. It's not just about maximising profits, it's about working within certain limits imposed upon us by the culture of the organisation. But you'd be doing pretty badly not to make a profit in Croke Park. We have the money coming in here, after all."

That means the major issue is what to do with the money you're getting in. Duffy acknowledges the tension between the big centre and the small club, as he puts it. "The arguments come in when you deal with the distribution of that revenue. Do you put it into coaching and games? Do you say no matter what, do you put it into infrastructure? We have some huge challenges in that area. We've just committed £15 million sterling to the redevelopment of Casement Park; Pairc Uí Chaoimh is coming and clearly we're going to have to invest significantly in that stadium, which is going to have to be redeveloped or else it'd have to be closed.

"A lot of income will go on those projects, not to mention the need for a smaller venue in the Dublin area. Then you have to ask, how will that affect investment in the coaching and games end? That constant debate is always there between the big centre and the small club."

——

Take TV rights. TV money is the big revenue generator for professional sports around the world, obviously. From the Premiership in England to the major leagues in America, the broadcasting deal is the one that pays the bills.

Duffy points out that differences in population make comparisons invidious, but that's not to say there isn't big money floating around. (The general figure most observers settle for is a total of approximately €10 million per annum, all in, though everybody—on all sides of the negotiating table—is reluctant to go on the record with an exact figure.) Clearly in an environment where the Premier League secured TV rights for over £3 billion, that figure's small feed. But given that there are no shareholders to pay off or players earning a quarter of a million pounds per week, it can all be deployed directly for the improvement of standards all round.

"Our TV rights are valuable, but in comparison with sports abroad they're absolutely tiny," says Duffy. "I had lunch with Andrew Demetriou of the AFL the last time we were out in Australia, and we're not comparable sports because they're professional and we're not. They have a tender process, an auction, and they try to get every cent they can.

"With our TV rights we're constrained, rightly, because we wouldn't get away with selling the rights to the championship to Sky Sports or somebody like that, even though those organisations have expressed an interest. With us, we start from this point—how can we best promote the games and make them available to the maximum number of people? It's after those criteria are addressed that we think about maximising the revenue from those."

The revelation that a satellite broadcaster is interested in GAA coverage would provoke two simultaneous and contradictory responses in most GAA people: delight at increased revenue and unease at the move to pay-per-view. Duffy says it's not a runner at present anyway.

"It's a help to the situation that TV3 have developed an interest in the GAA, but clearly its resources are limited. So it'd be very difficult for us to cut our ties completely to RTÉ even if we wanted to. As I say, we've had informal approaches from satellite broadcasters, but we can't go that way, really. Whatever you might like to say, and you might like to say otherwise, essentially the membership wouldn't allow you to do that.

"I could go out tomorrow and Sky will offer us four or five times what RTÉ are offering, but I know if I came back to management with that, the organisation would say to me, 'Get out of here. We're not doing that.' We have Setanta in for the national league, fair enough, but in terms of maximising our return from media or TV rights, we can't do that in the way that other organisations can, like the IRFU or the FAI could."

The director-general doesn't see objections to satellite companies like Sky being based, necessarily, on the view that it could end up influencing match scheduling, as has happened in the Premiership. The unease with the powerful broadcaster is more to do with access to its services, though Duffy concedes that that's not as powerful an argument as it might have been even a few years ago.

"I don't think that would be the issue, though it hasn't gone that far. I think the issue would be taking the games off free-to-air broadcasting. There's a sense that the GAA belongs to everybody in Ireland, that it's in every parish and village, and that there'd be enormous resistance if we were to take the games off free-to-air, even though the majority of the population probably has access to Sky. But as long as 10 per cent of the population don't have access to Sky, I don't think the organisation would tolerate more than, say, the amount covered by Setanta not being on free-to-air. I just don't think the tolerance is there for anything other than free-to-air in the short term."

———

One of the men who sat alongside Duffy to negotiate the TV deal with RTÉ the last time out agrees with the director-general on the pay-per-view issue. Former GAA president Christy Cooney concedes that a deal with a satellite TV company would bring in a multiple of the money paid by RTÉ, but as he says, economics isn't everything.

"That's true in terms of the economics," says Cooney, "but the job is to get enough to continue to reinvent the Association, to support the development of our games, our infrastructural requirements and to increase participation levels. We need to have every person in Ireland able to access our games; we could never see a situation where a Munster football final or a Leinster hurling final would not be free to people to see it. It's not about money—it's about getting enough revenue in to sustain our games.

"We're not a professional sport. Rugby and soccer are totally different in that sense. The money is necessary for us, but it's not the ultimate. The ultimate is to raise participation, and money isn't the be-all and end-all. I would never be in favour of signing away our soul, our rights, to an international broadcaster who would control us in terms of how we go forward.

"We do a portion with Setanta; we support TG4, who are in turn a fantastic support to us; RTÉ have always done a good job and TV3 are an Irish company, so we have created competition in the Irish sector. If they want to compete for our games that's great, but people can still access our games free to air. That's the way it should be."

Cooney concedes that the rising tide of live TV coverage didn't lift all boats; some games are just not going to draw in viewers compared to other, sexier match-ups, so the GAA did something about that. It cut games from the schedule.

"Now, we took a decision to reduce the number of games from 50 to 40 on TV because some games weren't getting the audiences, and weren't as attractive, and were affecting the club scene. Of course we can do better—if we tighten the time frame of our championships that would help viewing figures, too. We probably need to expand the colleges coverage over the next few years. I think there's potential there. But we don't need to saturate TV with our games, because most of all we want footfall. We want people to come to the games—families, kids, all of that."

――――

For an illustration of how activities on the field feed into broadcasting rights, by the way, consider the importance of one county's success in 2011 and its significance for future TV deals. A general question to

Páraic Duffy on the impact of Dublin's All-Ireland win leads to one specific area where the team Pat Gilroy managed to glory produced a very specific dividend.

"It's good for the game because most of the media are based in Dublin; there's a glamour attached—the Man United of the GAA— and people have a love-hate attitude to them. Apart from Pat Gilroy's first year, Dublin's gates are no bigger now than they were eight to ten years ago—they'll always attract good gates, obviously, because of the numbers here. In terms of the finances, they are important and we need them. Obviously if they went down and ended up in Division Two or Three that would have a major impact, but it's been pretty static over the last ten or 12 years, apart from that one bad year.

"However, one key point is that their games attract big television viewing figures. If you look at TV3 they'll take as many Dublin games as they can because they know they'll get the viewing figures—and the advertising revenue. RTÉ will go around the provinces but TV3, every chance they get, will show Dublin.

"The three biggest TV audiences last year on RTÉ were the two All-Ireland finals and the Donegal-Dublin game in the championship. That's significant. They're good for us, and they're good for TV. If you ask RTÉ or TV3 they'll tell you that Dublin are the team they want to be successful because they'll bring in the viewing figures and they'll bring in the advertising. And for us it adds to the value of the TV contract: if Dublin were unsuccessful that would have a huge impact on the contract because of the huge viewing figures they attract."

That contract is up for renewal this year. Duffy's candour suggests that a resurgent Dublin—under new boss Jim Gavin—would be of huge benefit to the GAA when they sit down with RTÉ to renegotiate, but those discussions are expected to be a good deal tougher in any case. The country's economic situation guarantees that.

"The last deal we did we'd be generally happy with," says Cooney. "Myself and Páraic would have managed that with Dermot Power. Bearing in mind the economic challenges, I think we did very well, but it'll be tougher the next time. That means we have to look at things differently, where we want to go with those rights. Do we want to look at our own international television opportunities, through our website, other companies, through our own tech TV—how would that work in terms of being economically viable? Would we get advertising for that?

"Generally I think we're in a good space—what we have, the public wants to watch, so companies are prepared to sponsor and advertise. We have very good partners with the likes of Musgraves, with Centra, Etihad, Eircom—they wouldn't be with us unless it was beneficial for their business. So that means our brand has a lot to offer, and we have to be positive about that always."

There's a practical aspect to those relationships, adds Cooney.

"That isn't just the brand at inter-county level, it applies at local level too. Will people go to shop at Centra instead of Tesco because they're associated with the GAA? I believe they will. Otherwise those companies wouldn't be with us. We're in a good space, but we need to keep looking at things and make decisions that are in our interests.

"Take radio. We've moved into Newstalk, which is great, but local radio in particular is something we can't do without. People listen to those stations to keep abreast of club developments, and that's as important as TV rights. It's community-driven, which ties in with our ethos."

That's the GAA's view of its relationship with the major broadcaster in the country. But what about RTÉ's view of that relationship?

Chapter 17 ⌒

A MARRIAGE OF LIKE MINDS: RTÉ AND THE GAA: MEDIA RIGHTS II

We referred in our last chapter, also on media rights, to comments from Seán Kelly MEP about RTÉ's coverage of the GAA. It's worth revisiting some other comments from the former GAA president in that context, particularly his view that there was a sense that "the very fact of our games being amateur means that they are somehow less worthy of notice".

Kelly expanded his point, however, beyond simply criticising the State broadcaster. For instance, he wanted more coverage of the weaker football and hurling counties, who don't always get their day in the sun: "I'd like to see more of the big teams featured but also more of the other teams as well. They're all performing pro rata at the top level. It's only their populations that are holding small counties back. They can't achieve what big counties can achieve because of their size, but that's not to say what they're doing is not worthy of recognition. There are so many channels available now anyway and we should be giving priority to what is unique and distinctive to our country particularly when it concerns our own sportsmen and sportswomen."

Kelly also described his disappointment at the scant coverage now given to the lower hurling inter-county championships. "Sometimes they cover the basics, a couple of minutes of most games that you would probably expect to see covered far more extensively. For instance, the Christy Ring and Nicky Rackard Cups that were introduced when I was president, they don't get any coverage at all at the moment. That's a combination of years of work in planning and training and they're the highlight of careers for many of those players. They deserve their coverage. It can't just be about the big counties."

True to his word as president, when he opened Croke Park to soccer and rugby, Kelly takes a broad view of sport as a force for good on television. "As far as I'm concerned the more sport the better. We are recognised as being a sporting country. We talk about being world class in certain sports and our sports people have shown that more than anyone. Particularly nowadays, with so many challenges facing young people, we want to see more people involved in sport and certainly seeing our heroes on the national broadcasters can be a great contributory factor to that. Sport contributes more than these un-reality TV programmes, as I call them. They're called reality programmes but they're the most unreal of all kinds."

In a statement released to the *Irish Examiner* at the time of Kelly's comments, RTÉ admitted the "current financial climate" had impacted on their coverage of Gaelic games. I thought RTÉ might like to give a bit more background to that.

———

A knowledgeable man with a well-developed awareness of how both organisations function once described the GAA-RTÉ relationship as something like a difficult marriage, adding that RTÉ couldn't do without the GAA and vice versa.

It's a compelling thesis, given the huge ratings RTÉ enjoys when it comes to the All-Ireland series, and the vast coverage across all platforms, to use the current jargon, that RTÉ affords the championships in particular, even during a summer like 2012 when there were Olympic Games and European Championships jostling for attention.

I put that to Ryle Nugent, RTÉ Head of Sport, but first I addressed whether the GAA has grounds for feeling it's not adequately served by RTÉ.

"I wouldn't say it's a specific GAA issue. All sport struggles, to varying degrees, with how they deal with the media, and television specifically, and how that fits into their overall plans. I don't think it'd be fair to single out the GAA particularly for having a difficult relationship with any broadcaster.

"In an overall sense it's about marrying the requirements of the sport, the financial rewards of that sport through media rights and keeping the bloke who's paid you the money happy for what he's paid for. In any walk of life that can be a difficult balance to strike, so I don't think it's specific to the GAA. Having said that, regarding the GAA, we have a very good working relationship with them, and that's not a PR position. It's a factual position."

Nugent acknowledges that some of the challenges the two bodies face may arise from simple similarity. They're two of the largest organisations in Ireland and have a similar, lengthy reach into every corner of the island, but the RTÉ man teases out those likenesses: "In many ways there are some similarities between the two organisations in terms of structure, in terms of the GAA's internal tension between an amateur ethos and a professional attitude, while we have the public service and commercial challenge. That's not a dissimilar situation, so I think we understand each other even when there's frustration there; that it isn't just about cold, hard cash for anybody. There are requirements to recognise the multifaceted elements that both the GAA and RTÉ are part of.

"In terms of the relationship on a day-to-day basis, Liam (O'Neill), Páraic (Duffy), Peter (McKenna) and Lisa (Clancy) are the people we'd deal with and they're very practical. They have their own difficulties, but I'd like to think they'd say the same about us, and recognise that we have our difficulties too. The relationship is good. A marriage isn't a bad way to describe it, but it's a happy marriage at the moment."

———

Nugent's point that most sports organisations tend to gravitate towards a certain amount of dissatisfaction with their levels of coverage is one that'll ring true with anyone who works in a sports-related branch of the media. Every sport wants more coverage, and uncritical coverage at that.

Nugent points to unfair comparisons with broadcasters across the water, however, stressing that it's not a matter of like with like.

"Of course, rightly or wrongly RTÉ is lined up in direct comparison with the likes of the BBC, ITV and Sky. I have no problem with that. I think those comparisons have driven a lot of what's good about RTÉ sport because you have those benchmarks there to drive us to be as good as we can be despite having only a fraction of the staff and finance those organisations have.

"The flip side is that we're not Sky because we're not a sports channel. People forget that very quickly. We're not a BBC or ITV because you're talking about a population of 60 million compared to a population here of 4.5 million. The BBC licence fee is monumental in comparison to RTÉ's. You're talking £3.6 billion versus €183.6 million in 2011. The comparison with ITV on commercial terms isn't fair either.

"What we've tried to do in RTÉ to differentiate ourselves—something which has been done for many years before me and which I'm trying to continue—is to establish an editorial line of our people calling it as they see it. We do that with our GAA coverage, with our soccer coverage and with our rugby coverage.

"Do we always get it right? No. Is there always room for improvement? Absolutely. Would we be arrogant enough to think we have a God-given right to get the audience to join us? Absolutely not. We have to fight for that like everybody else. Don't forget there's huge choice here in a tiny market, very little if anything is now truly exclusive—BBC, ITV, Sky, TV3, Setanta, TG4, ESPN. That's very competitive."

It also illustrates the range of options open to sports organisations, including the GAA. When Nugent points out that those choices are available to all sports organisations, including the GAA, he adds that some have availed of those choices, including the GAA. He admits that the notion of the GAA's dependence on the State broadcaster is "oversold", and the evidence does seem to back him up.

"Whether it's the GAA, the IRFU, the FAI, athletics, racing or boxing," says Nugent, "they're all engaged with us to get the best they can get from us. And that's what I'd expect. But with the GAA it's important to remember that they, like all rights holders, do have a choice and have exercised that choice. We're conscious of that. The belief that the GAA can't exist without RTÉ is oversold, I think.

"The GAA has clearly signalled that by selling a package or two of championship rights to TV3, and league rights to TG4 and Setanta. This isn't a complaint by any stretch of the imagination, by the way, but the suggestion that RTÉ can march in arrogantly and demand X, Y and Z simply isn't true."

———

The RTÉ man also acknowledges the public service remit as feeding directly into the coverage of smaller counties' games. It's obviously not a consideration for a hard-nosed commercial operation, but RTÉ must cover games at times which are, to be blunt, unattractive propositions.

"We do have that remit and it is important we don't just focus on one team or group," says Nugent. "We also have an editorial focus which, by its nature, comes to a natural conclusion with quarter, semi-finals and finals. But the other side of that is there are very few games that do badly for us, and that doesn't fall along county lines. There's a connection between the general audience and GAA coverage. Kerry v Dublin or Kilkenny v Tipperary in the latter end of the championship will be bigger than a first-round qualifier game, fair enough, but a first-round Euro 2012 game will not be as big as the final either when it comes to audience size. As a competition comes to a climax, the floating viewer will come in while the core audience is engaged no matter what. That's true across all sports."

What's also changed across all sports—all areas of life—is the monetary landscape. When you nudge the RTÉ boss about the broadcasting negotiations this year (2013), he points out that the lesson of the downturn is that everyone's had to learn—and one that everybody brings to the negotiating table.

"That reality is there for everybody. This isn't something that I'll land in to negotiate with Páraic and Peter, and we'll all be shocked by it. Everybody is dealing with this already and we've dealt with other organisations with this in mind as well. From the smallest business to the biggest there's been a sea change in attitudes, and everybody has to figure out how to move forward—unless you're the FA in England and you land a £3 billion deal for three years, which defies logic!

"I think the GAA, RTÉ, the FAI, the IRFU, every business, you name it, every organisation knows the country has changed and that therefore the rules and regulations under which deals are collectively constructed have changed. You always need to centre this as not just a GAA issue, but an issue for every sports organisation or association. It's up to each of those bodies to decide what they bring to the market, and as an example, there was a fundamental change in the number of games covered in this contract compared to the previous deal. That wasn't because of RTÉ—or TV3, or TG4, or Setanta—but it was because the GAA decides how it sells its games, as is right and proper. That's the first thing.

"When we see what's on offer, and the amount of money we bring to the negotiation, then we see how we're going to approach it. Look at the European soccer championships, which changed from a 16-team to a 24-team format. The GAA might bring in a structural change—I don't know if they will or not, but they're entitled to do that, obviously, and I wouldn't try to second-guess what any association will bring to the table. You must deal with it as you find it."

Back to the significance of the championship structure: the predictability of attractive fixtures, and how that could be marketed to sponsors and broadcasters, is something that figures prominently in other parts of this book. Clearly a structure which would allow RTÉ plenty of notice in terms of build-up would benefit the broadcaster and the GAA alike.

The relationship between the two big beasts of Irish popular culture still functions well, for all the shadow-boxing that might be looming on the horizon. Nugent's brief goes far beyond head-scratchers such as which obscure football qualifier to cover on an overcast Saturday in July, and he's at pains—understandably—to put the GAA in the context of what RTÉ have to do for all sports in the country. He adds, though, that RTÉ are also about giving the audience what it wants.

"I'm happy with what we've brought to the table in terms of our overall ethos. They're our national games and the championship gets the due recognition it deserves from the national broadcaster, I think," says Nugent. "The All-Ireland finals are still, every year, two of the top ten most-watched programmes and the championship is engaged with all through the summer, even in the face of competition from the Euros and other events. It has its rightful place in the Irish psyche and we're about giving the audience what it wants, so the championship has its rightful place with us, too. We'll continue working with the GAA on various projects like Hawkeye, analysis tools and so on.

"Do we get it right all the time? No. We work a lot on what we can do and we're always in development; it's fluid."

Chapter 18

WHEN SPORTS SUCCESS IS BAD FOR BUSINESS: ANATOMY OF A SPONSORSHIP

Why do companies get involved with GAA sponsorship? What's in it for them apart from having their brand name splashed across a jersey or their firm's colours dangling from a cup?

It's easy to say that the GAA is a vibrant organisation and companies like to be associated with sports which engross hundreds of thousands every summer, but what's the bottom line? John Mullins, then CEO of Bord Gáis, considers that basic question: why did his company get into GAA sponsorship, and why did he select the U21 hurling championship in particular?

He sketches a context: "Take the business end of things first. Every business goes through cycles, some growth cycles and some retention cycles. Sponsorship, advertising and brand enhancement—and brand change—these are all done when you either want to acquire new customers or retain customers who are loyal to you. So your strategy is always going to move, which is why generally, with a few exceptions, companies won't stay with a particular sponsorship for more than three years. Now, recent GAA sponsorships have been longer—Guinness, Bank of Ireland, Etihad—but they're the exception.

"Venue sponsorship is very popular. Aviva wanted to change the Hibernian company name a couple of years ago: Hibernian was a very strong brand, but Aviva meant absolutely nothing to the Irish consumer. They felt that to retain and acquire (customers), the right thing to do was to carry out a study on whether Lansdowne Road should be called the Aviva. There must have been 20 companies mentioned as a venue sponsor, but what was needed was a value for money study."

Mullins wanted to reposition Bord Gáis when he took over; that entailed finding out how people perceived the company and identifying the tie-in which would help change that perception if it were counter-productive.

"Tracking back to where we were when I came in back in 2007, we had a brand that was clunky, that was masculine, that didn't have any form of relevance to the people who paid the bills, so we needed to look at a variety of sponsorships and brand enhancements to change that. Sport is only one part of that, because community involvement, arts and theatre, events like festivals—all of that is involved. Because we're a national brand we wanted to be as relevant as possible, so I set up a sponsorship steering committee to look into it, and we brought in John Trainor of Onside Sponsorship to advise us."

Because Bord Gáis Energy (BGE) was viewed as an urban company with a generally masculine image, the GAA was the ideal partner to help Mullins tweak that. "You look at what your customer base is interested in, and we'd get information from our bill payers that some are involved in the GAA, which was important as an urban company—which we are—if you wanted to connect with rural people. So going in at U21 level made absolute sense. But we tested all that, and we'd have tested for the last three years how we'd done with that sponsorship. John (Trainor) would evaluate all the sponsorship packages out there and would have a ranking order of effectiveness."

Bord Gáis didn't put all their eggs in one basket either: "We needed to be relevant to mná na hÉireann as well, so one of the things we did was to redesign our logo—to feminise it—and we went into book clubs. We renamed the Grand Canal Theatre, and there are two points there that arose in our analysis—that women were more inclined to book the tickets and go to the theatre, and we also wanted to create a rewards club, a mini-Groupon idea, so that BGE customers would remain loyal to the brand. That's the retention part I mentioned earlier."

And they turned to ladies' football, sponsoring the national leagues in that sport.

"That's been a real success for us, particularly in the regional press—they're covering their local team on a regular basis and mentioning the BGE league. The U21 championship is more of a national event and you have to put in your time with the launches, with Ger (Cunningham) working with the captains, so there's a lot of work that goes into it. The ladies' football has been a huge success. You have TG4 for the whole day, when you think of it, for the finals, and it's one of the fastest-growing sports in the country. The people who run it are top class—they certainly run a great All-Star night."

BGE don't sponsor a sports venue, but the chief executive offers a cash value for their theatre sponsorship which sets the background for the company's major GAA sponsorship deal.

"Regarding venue sponsorship, it's a major thing to get your name on a venue which has maybe 800,000 people going through it every year: the name is on the venue, on the ticket, on the radio . . . it's on everything. The media value we calculated for the BGE Theatre is somewhere in the region of €13 to €15 million. The science is about your customer's view of what you do, and then the amount of media exposure your platform gets. We find that GAA correspondents are very loyal to launches for the U21 championship, so there's a dividend in that."

———

That loyalty is easy to understand when you consider the quality of the fare on offer in the U21 hurling championship in recent years, but when it came to sponsoring that grade, one extra element to BGE's consideration of sponsorship wasn't necessarily business-based.

Mullins himself went to the North Monastery, a famous cradle of hurling in Cork city, and played the game to a high standard himself. He recognised something innately attractive in the U21 hurling championship, something that wouldn't have been obvious to someone with no understanding of the game.

"As someone who played hurling I'd have understood that the U21 grade is one of the purest forms of the game—there's less cynicism, which has been borne out in recent years. That's one point. Other than that, if you want to be relevant in sports sponsorship in Ireland, the GAA is an important part of that. We looked at the All-Ireland league in rugby, but it was dying on its feet. We'd been involved in the League of Ireland before—for many years—and we looked at other sports. We sponsored the Cork City Marathon, for instance, but that was as much about volunteering as the race, about community involvement as much as the competition itself. So we went with the U21 hurling championship."

Early on they struck publicity gold. The first game Mullins went to was the Clare-Tipperary Munster final in Ennis in 2010, a tight game which was won by Tipperary because the umpire called the attention of the referee to the Clare keeper stepping outside the small parallelogram late on. The referee awarded a 65 to punish the infraction, calling back the play from the other end of the field, where Clare were just about to point the free that would have given them their first title in the grade.

Deprived at the very death of a historic victory, the Clare supporters at Cusack Park didn't react well. There were sensational photographs in the newspapers the next day of gardaí accompanying the match officials off the field, right through an angry mob which wasn't shy about making its feelings known. Chaos and uproar.

"There was a small riot," laughs Mullins. "I couldn't present the trophy. Jimmy O'Gorman, the Munster Council chairman, presented it. But it was some start: it created notoriety for the grade."

That was an unexpected bonus and an early return on their investment. Generally speaking that investment requires a lot more hard work to make it count, says the chief executive.

"The economics of a sports sponsorship are that you buy your rights but you must pay at least a similar amount to market it. In a three-year deal you pay most in the first year, less in the second and less in the third, but you should see the return in that investment coming through.

"How do you quantify the return? We ask focus groups, 'are you more or less likely to buy Bord Gáis products because of A, B or C', and what we found was that while the U21 hurling championship mightn't sound like a great sponsorship in itself, we would have seen it as a top-12 product in the country from our work with John [Trainor]. We had progressively moved it on with the ambassador idea with Joe Canning, blogs and social media—all with a view to getting a younger audience involved, and also, clearly, to give it some notoriety. You're still doing old media, of course, and we also needed someone who knew his way around. Ger Cunningham was ideal, so I took him out of his old job and put him in there. You've got to invest internally as well as externally."

You can't legislate for results, but Mullins points to the dividend BGE has enjoyed as a result of variety on the winners' podium. He also adds that although many people laud Kilkenny for their excellence as they've dominated the senior grade for the last decade—including Paudie Butler in this book—in strict business terms the Cats' bullying of an entire generation of opponents is a disincentive to potential sponsors. If the result's a foregone conclusion, that reduces the level of interest.

"We've been fortunate as well, I have to say, in that every year we've sponsored the competition we've had a different champion, which is always good. My own view on the senior hurling championship, for what it's worth, was that I wasn't so sure I wanted to sponsor the senior hurling championship when there was one dominant party."

———

Along the way both organisations have swapped ideas. Mullins points to technological innovations which have run in parallel with classic games.

"I was at the Cork-Limerick U21 final in 2011, which will be remembered for the hurling, but for me it'll also be the first game I was able to get a QR code from a programme for a smartphone and was then able to pick up a couple of videos of captains talking about the final.

"I was in Sisco in Silicon Valley recently and they're all talking about enabling smartphones at stadiums. The programmes of the future will be available on your smartphone, and I told this to some people in the GAA and I might as well have been speaking double Dutch, but I think there is progressive modernisation in the Association. Take Guinness's sponsorship of the Irish rugby team, with little games for Iphone. Those little games add to the rights that you buy."

Mullins sees the GAA moving forward in terms of social media, but he advises the organisation to listen to its own members. Not so much the county board delegates or the full-time officials who make the strategic decisions, but the tech-savvy kids on various U14 and U15 teams, if someone can tear them away from their technology.

"You're always looking for new ways to connect. The sports organisation is giving you a platform from which you create product, and progressively over the last few years the GAA has opened up what is possible in terms of social media. They understand more than anyone else that their target audience is made up of 13 and 14-year-old kids with their smartphones. They'll do more with those than the president of the GAA will ever do, no matter who he is.

"The GAA, for its future survival, will have to be aware of these young kids, the 'millennials', who socialise on Facebook, Twitter, LinkedIn and so on. The whole world of marketing has changed fundamentally. I was at a conference recently and a Google VP who was there said that if you're not on the above sites, or Google Plus, then you don't exist."

Mullins, who has an All-Ireland colleges football medal in the far recesses of an impressive CV, also recognises the particular challenge of the GAA: that it doesn't—and can't—jump into bed with just any business partner.

"To be fair to the GAA, they won't just take on any company— they'll only take on a company in line with its own ethos. We're a national company and we were able to leverage the U21 with the 'Big Switch' campaign, and it tied in with our social media work. But then you need to activate intelligently, to get the best guys around to get your product to grow, and I'd like to think we brought new tricks and new approaches to the GAA that hadn't been tried before. And we learned new tricks as well along the way."

He's happy to share those ideas with the Association. Take the model for the All-Ireland finals offered by last year's SuperBowl to follow: "The 2012 Superbowl was the first that was fully web-enabled—the only problem in the stadium was that the coaches' headsets were creating interference on the broadband signal in the front-row seats, but that was fixed.

"Once you got into your app, you were able to see replays, different angles—all at the touch of a button—with an ad in the middle of it. In ten years' time you'll be going to Croke Park with an Ipad or Google goggles with the same experience. There are plenty of challenges to the GAA in terms of players, and the issue is to stay relevant for my son, who's playing under 13. He's interested in what the GAA tells him on Facebook because he doesn't watch TV.

"The notion that he does what he's told by the 2D box in the corner—forget it. The GAA needs to be about propagating messaging using various sources to reach that clientele. Which is what we were trying to do with the 'Energy to break through' campaign—we insisted on a playercam for the All-Ireland final, and TG4 wants to push the boat out on this. What's the GAA plan to ensure a Sky-type experience?"

Mullins adds that the ball is in the Association's court; it's up to the GAA to take the initiative.

"I'd hope they'd be ahead of the curve with that—and at the same time to make that experience available to the 15-year old with his Ipad, and to make training video clips available to coaches—at no massive cost. Take everything that's being done in other sports and try to make it available in new media. The GAA's in competition with other sports, and if they're not successful, then companies like ours will go elsewhere."

Chapter 19

BEYOND THE BORDER: POPULARITY OUTSIDE THE COUNTY

The jerseys and hoodies, the t-shirts and baseball caps. The visibility of branded merchandise, the rolling coverage on TV and radio, the reams of newspaper interviews and features . . . at times in the summer the GAA championships seem to be everywhere.

And anywhere the championship is visible, so are sponsors. They must be laughing all the way to the bank with that kind of exposure.

Aren't they?

————

John Trainor of Onside Sponsorship explains what his firm does.

"We supply business facts and figures to the decision-making process. Typically we sit on the sponsors' side of the fence and would work with the premier brands in the market, some of whom are investing seven-figure sums. As a result they need to be certain their decisions are built on robust facts and figures.

"In working with businesses we try to establish whether sponsorship is right for their business and what they should spend—within their overall marketing budget—on sports sponsorship compared to other forms of marketing. When they reach that point we help them to move on and seek out sponsorship that's right for them and which will fit in with what they're trying to achieve.

"Different companies have different target markets, different objectives and so on, so the shopping lists can be relatively different. We tend to get to a point where, if they say it's sport, we say, 'Well, is it GAA or rugby or golf or whatever?'

"That's where they decide what sponsorship opportunities within those sports they'd like to buy and we take them to a point where we help them negotiate the best deal they can get and put the contracts in place."

So far so good, but while that's admirable in a general sense, can Trainor and his colleagues quantify the benefits—potential and actual—of a good sponsorship? Is it a science with measurable outcomes? Turns out it is.

"This is all grounded in good relationships we have with the rights-holders in the markets," says Trainor. "When we come to the table to explore possibilities, we know what the rights-holders want, what they're looking for and how their businesses and organisations work. We're sensitive that approaches are made in the proper manner, that there's a link between the corporate brand or business and often a rights-holder who's less corporate in how they view their organisations.

"We're trying to be the conduit between the two, so that when there's interaction between them that that takes place in the right way. That's key—if the relationship starts well, it'll go well, and if not it doesn't. So we bring a lot of stats and figures in order to bring certainty to the sponsor—the ultimate tag-line is to 'partner with confidence'. If you want me to put a number on it, I would say that within five to ten per cent either way we can give them certainty on how a sponsorship will perform for a business."

———

The figures don't end there. Trainor has an array of statistics at his fingertips which show the bottom line when it comes to successful commercial partnerships within the GAA.

"That's how we've built our business. We're able to identify the number of people, say, who'd be aware of a sponsor. If someone wanted to sponsor the Cork hurlers in the morning we could tell them what they'd get in terms of awareness, the amount of people who'd feel differently or more positive about the company because of that sponsorship.

"We spend a lot of time determining how good the fit is, because that'll determine how successful it is on the other side—the stronger the fit at the outset in the public mind the more successful that sponsorship will be. The weaker the fit and the consumer ends up scratching his head and saying 'I don't get that.' If that happens then the sponsorship tends not to perform as strongly."

There are different ways of evaluating the success of sponsorship, he adds: "Within the industry traditionally the way to quantify sponsorship has been to look at media value. A lot of people in the industry would have used the 'how many column inches did you get and what media value would you put on that' as the measurement. We're of a different school of thought in that while that's one measurement, for us it's not purely about the outputs generated through exposure, it's about the outcomes of that exposure.

"By that I mean we look at how many people actually see that sponsorship and how many of those feel differently about the brand because of the sponsorship?"

First things first, then: where does the GAA rank as an entity within the Irish sports/commercial community? Very highly, says Trainor.

———

"We tend to base our perspectives on research," he says. "The fact is that if you ask the public what their favourite sponsorship of the last 12 months was, then for the last number of years, looking at different areas, then the GAA has been the one most frequently identified as the one most people will say, 'this brand sponsors X in the GAA and that's my favourite sponsorship'.

"In terms of its overall standing within the market, it and rugby have become, jointly, the two areas which command the appeal of half the country. In terms of general public appeal, GAA sponsorships are top within the market in terms of public appeal.

"Another metric we use is one where we talk to sponsors on an annual basis and ask what areas they see as the best value sponsorship opportunities, and GAA and rugby are numbers one and two in the market and have been consistently over recent years."

Being confined, more or less, to the island of Ireland has its advantages, says Trainor. "Sometimes there's criticism that the GAA is somewhat cluttered, slightly busy, in terms of the number of brands, but in my view it has the potential to be a little cleaner than other platforms because it's Irish.

"By that I mean if I want to sponsor soccer, I'll have to compete with the multiple brands involved in local soccer, local rugby and so on, as well as all the international brands operating in that space. If you're operating in the GAA market you're only competing with the other GAA sponsors, though, and that's a strength within the market. It's something that would strike a sponsor trying to stand out within a market getting busier all the time.

"The GAA uniquely provides a relatively genuine national footprint. We have research showing that about 55 per cent of the country would be interested in the GAA to some degree, which demonstrates a broad national footprint. And as it does become a numbers game for many brands, that's a key number."

————

Trainor continues: "If I were talking to a colleague in England, what I'd be telling him is that in Ireland at the moment there are 670,000 Man Utd fans, 535,000 Dublin Gaelic football fans, 456,000 Liverpool fans, 422,000 Cork hurling fans, 399,000 Dublin hurling fans, 339,000 Kilkenny hurling fans, 336,000 Cork football fans and 239,000 Tipperary fans.

"The point is that in the Irish market the Dublin Gaelic footballers and hurlers and the Cork Gaelic footballers and hurlers command bigger support bases, or bases as big, as any Premiership team outside Liverpool and Man Utd. There are significantly more Cork and Dublin fans than there are for Chelsea or Arsenal, for instance, which shows the scale and size of the fan bases which support their counties."

Trainor's stats show that the potential appeal of some counties spills over their natural boundaries: "If you ask people the question, 'my number one county football team is . . . ' then 20 per cent of the people who say Cork live outside Cork, while 28 per cent of the people whose favourite hurling team is Cork live outside the county.

"So there's a real value to be gained outside a county from partnering with a county itself. A company like Esat Digifone, and later O2, would have strategically followed an approach which allowed Cork to become the foundation for their growth within Ireland as a business, and on that logic I could see how a brand which may not be fully established nationally but would have aspirations to do so, out of a Cork base, would use a similar model to Esat Digifone."

Trainor sees stronger partnership between the GAA, its commercial partners and supporters as the way forward. "Thinking with my sponsorship hat on, I think facilitating greater interaction between sponsors and fans at grass-roots level, whatever structure that would take, would help. Companies are looking beyond sponsorship to try to build affinity between the sponsor and the brand, and now they're trying to see what greater commercial opportunities may exist—say, affinity schemes or mechanics to get sponsors doing business directly with fans, where fans show loyalty to sponsors who support their teams.

"If there were some way to facilitate that for sponsors then it's something that would appeal to those sponsors, because that's what they're looking for—it shows a real benefit."

What's the logical next step, then? Trainor reaches across the Atlantic for his example.

"The NASCAR support base is always showcased as the industry textbook case of fans who support sponsors—the perfect model of how fans are willing to do that. I think supporters are open to greater levels of commercialism, to greater levels of activation. I don't think the GAA is getting close to the ceiling of what can be done, and there's the possibility of an opportunity to extend the degree of fan interaction in terms of commercial opportunities.

"There's a growing appetite for sports, but we see that many of the people now following sports are more casual than avid fans, and those casual fans aren't purely interested in the beauty of the game. They may be there for entertainment, so they have an appetite in GAA—and other sports—for other entertainment that they may be willing to pay for, and that entertainment may not be limited to what's going on in the game.

"The GAA has recognised the opportunities here with the Family Fun Zone and other initiatives in Croke Park and elsewhere. I don't see consumer resistance to those; on the contrary, I think people enjoy them and those supporters who are GAA fans but who are also rugby and soccer fans may notice if those activities are not there when they go to GAA games. I think there'll be more of that in the future and that it'll be well received by the public.

"How far will it go? I think the GAA probably has a chance to steal a march in terms of its partnerships with companies/brands because sponsorships are at a turning point and companies/brands are looking for new types of activities. And the GAA has a good chance to lead that kind of initiative and to go beyond the traditional models."

That may begin with the most basic item that's sponsored . . . "I'm surprised that GAA jerseys aren't more central to the involvement of sponsors. In the States some sports teams have badges on the sleeve of their supporters' jerseys which have microchips embedded to facilitate getting a burger or a beer, say, at the stadium. As a fan it allows you to carry out business within the stadium.

"There are opportunities there for the GAA to set itself up as an innovator and pioneer, not trying to be smart and clever in itself, but trying to benefit everybody—the Association, the supporters and the teams."

John Trainor: "The GAA—a genuinely national footprint." (© *David Maher/SPORTSFILE*)

Jim Power: "There are some GAA activities which make no economic sense whatsoever." (© *Eric Luke/ Irish Times*)

John Considine: "Nobody gets rich working for the GAA." (© *INPHO/James Crombie*)

Tom Ryan: "About 86 per cent of the revenue people pay at the turnstiles is recycled within the GAA." (© *INPHO/James Crombie*)

Enda McGuane: "Concerts? Once people hear about concerts, kids running riot, they think, 'Do we really need that?'" (© *Brendan Moran/ SPORTSFILE*)

Mick O'Keeffe (with Kelli O'Keeffe): "The GAA skirts a line between professional sport and being a not-for-profit organisation." (© *Lazarov/Photocall Ireland*)

Peter McKenna: "Croke Park is debt-free." (© *INPHO/Cathal Noonan*)

Páraic Duffy: "It's not just about maximising profit; it's about working within certain limits imposed by the culture of the GAA." (© *INPHO/Dan Sheridan*)

The front of the Dublin jersey: the most lucrative spot in GAA advertising. (© *INPHO/Ryan Byrne*)

Before the revamp: Croke Park in the good old days. (© *GAA Archive*)

After the revamp: Croke Park under lights, 2007. (© *Stephen McCarthy/SPORTSFILE*)

Ryle Nugent: "A marriage isn't a bad way to describe it." (© *Brendan Moran/SPORTSFILE*)

Dessie Farrell: "The GAA has to be more confident in itself." (© *INPHO/Lorraine O'Sullivan*)

Paudie Butler: "Almost every child in the country wants to play hurley or camogie." (© *Brian Lawless/ SPORTSFILE*)

Dickie Murphy: "Making a draw of it? The last thing on a referee's mind." (© *INPHO/Morgan Treacy*)

Jack Anderson: "Fines? How effective are they?" (*Courtesy of Jack Anderson*)

Dónal Óg Cusack: "You wouldn't serve the individual very well if you brought him into a professional environment." (© *INPHO/ Lorraine O'Sullivan*)

Christy Cooney: "Outside managers don't happen in counties with a tradition of success." (© *INPHO/Lorraine O'Sullivan*)

Seán Kelly: "For small counties to close the gap would take huge effort. And huge resources." (© *INPHO/Lorraine O'Sullivan*)

The National League: standing room aplenty. (© *INPHO/Cathal Noonan*)

The Championship: packed to the rafters. (© INPHO/Cathal Noonan)

John Mullins: "The senior championship wasn't as attractive because one team was dominating." (© *Pat Murphy/SPORTSFILE*)

Croke Park, 1987: before the revamp—safety considerations. (© *Ray McManus/SPORTSFILE*)

Nickey Brennan: "If my club had to amalgamate, I'd be crying for a week." (© *INPHO/Morgan Treacy*)

Eamon O'Shea: "There is little in Irish life which is better value for money than membership of a GAA club." (© *Pat Murphy/SPORTSFILE*)

[Paudie Butler]: "We underestimated the damage done by giving bigger, heavier hurleys to children." (© *INPHO/Tom Honan*)

Chapter 20

BREAKFAST OF CHAMPIONS: HOW MUCH FOR A PLAYER TO ENDORSE YOUR PRODUCT?

There was a time within living memory when an inter-county player in either football or hurling wouldn't have been your first thought when it came to celebrity sports endorsement.

One or two broke out of the ghetto, true, but there was a suspicious consistency to the products they were associated with; they were generally of an agricultural bent, which reinforced a certain horny-handed, son-of-the-soil image. Drenches and mastitis figured prominently in the ad copy.

That's changed hugely. Now you see a GAA presence in, say, a McDonald's TV commercial, where a young boy getting a lift from his mother has a hurley and helmet under his arm, or a car insurance advertisement which shows a client hand-passing a football out of shot.

As for the players themselves . . . you can see hurlers and footballers advertising soft drinks alongside professional soccer players and rugby stars, endorsing banks and sports shops, top of the line sportswear like Adidas and Puma, Nike and Underarmour.

A zenith of sorts, or maybe a nadir, depending on your perspective, was reached when a famous American ice cream manufacturer saw the opportunity of a lifetime by linking themselves to Ben and Jerry O'Connor of Cork for obvious reasons.

On the one hand, it seems obvious to use some of the most recognisable sports people in a small country to advertise your wares, even if it seems to have taken marketing departments all over Ireland decades to reach that conclusion. But there's another reason GAA players are in vogue when it comes to promoting products. Cost.

———

Mick O'Keeffe's Pembroke Communications office overlooks Sir John Rogerson's Quay, floor-to-ceiling glass giving a fine view of the Irish Financial Services Centre and its environs across the Liffey. Pembroke is one of Dublin's top public relations firms and a visitor hauling around lazy assumptions in his back pocket about the interests of such a firm might be surprised to see the sliotar on a shelf, or a poster of U21 hurlers hanging on the wall.

The visitor would do well to park his prejudices: O'Keeffe, himself a former Dublin footballer, has worked with many hurlers and footballers on marketing and PR projects, and brings a clear-eyed honesty to the GAA player's place in the advertising world.

"Different guys suit different things, obviously," says O'Keeffe. "First of all they're very inexpensive, €1,000 to €1,500 for the day, particularly when compared to a rugby player, who'll cost between €3,000 to €5,000, or soccer players, who are largely unavailable anyway."

That's true, but O'Keeffe goes on to point out a fact that mars many a sports reporter's summer, though the public at large are unaware of it. Most inter-county players are unavailable to the media during the championship season unless it's a tightly controlled press call before a big championship game—or unless the player is pushing a particular product.

Keen-eyed consumers of media will note that often an in-depth interview with a star hurler or footballer comes with an accompanying line ("Johnny Murphy was speaking at the launch of SuperBog deodorant") and a photograph of the bold Johnny in a SuperBog-branded polo shirt. A fair exchange? Whether it is or not, O'Keeffe points out that the media's loss of access is public relations' gain.

"Because GAA players don't really talk to the media any more, that plays into PR hands—journalists only get to talk to them now when they're paid to be at events. The way our stuff is evaluated, quite crudely, is 'did you get a picture in the paper, did you get coverage?'

Looking at it that way, you could get €30,000 worth of media value for paying two footballers a couple of grand to turn up to an event.

"So what the GAA guys give is this: most of them are easy to work with, most of them are newsworthy from May to September anyway, and most of them are only available for interview at these paid-for gigs. So now there's almost an understanding between sports journalists, sports editors, PR agencies, players and brands that while there's a certain cost associated with setting these things up—photography and so on—you can run a pretty successful press conference for four or five grand and you'll get good value for money for that most of the time."

O'Keeffe is quick to point to the deal that changed the dynamic, and contrary to what you might think, it wasn't a player tie-in with a product. He also notes the correlation between on-field competitiveness and commercial desirability.

"There were some poor attempts at product placement back in the day, hurlers with sheep guns or whatever, but Guinness probably blazed the trail back in the nineties. They had a bit of luck in that you didn't have Kilkenny and Tipperary winning loads of All-Irelands at the time. Maybe interest wouldn't have been as great if they had. But you had 'Not Men But Giants', great campaigns. Then you had Bank of Ireland getting into the football, Adidas, Puma and Underarmour getting into GAA. It's become something of a no-brainer that for all of these you need to have a player or a number of players involved as ambassadors."

That's where the development has come for players. It's no longer a turn-up-and-here's-the-cheque. There's ongoing interaction between the company and the star. "In the last ten years you've gone from throwing a player into a photocall to a relationship," says O'Keeffe, "where he's an ambassador for the product, or he's exclusively associated with that product or he goes to corporate gigs. It's become more holistic. Take Ulster Bank. They've been giving players jobs, so they're there in work on the ground and they're available for those corporate gigs as well."

———

But while some players have become known by their first name, the ultimate level of recognition in Ireland—Henry, Seán Óg, Gooch—there's a hard commercial reality which means that the vast majority of inter-county players come nowhere near lucrative personal endorsement deals.

The GPA points out that it has 2,300 members, but invariably charities and businesses look for the same couple of dozen names, because those are the recognisable ones. O'Keeffe points out, in addition, that recognisability also owes something to the structure of the championships themselves.

"The problem with the GAA is that the way the championship is shaped, the promotion and marketing of players—and of the GAA itself—is directly linked to the fixtures. We have a very archaic fixture system, based on the provincial system, which is completely out of date. It's ludicrous really. What we need is a more defined season. What we need is a system where there's certainty for the players, for the media and for marketing purposes. One year Seán Cavanagh is hot; the next year no one wants to talk to him because Tyrone are gone early. One year Dessie Dolan is the player everyone wants to talk to, but then Westmeath go into a bit of a trough and they don't want to talk to him. There are five or six superstars and the rest come and go. At the moment you have the Gooch, and Donaghy is still there. The two Brogans. Seán Óg Ó hAilpín is still a superstar."

Then there are the people looking for those stars: this is where the relative surprise at encountering GAA merchandise sprinkled around Pembroke's offices comes in, because you're expecting the totems of south County Dublin middle class—rugby scarves, maybe, or a shopping bag from Hollister in the Dundrum Shopping Centre. When you say this to O'Keeffe he laughs but concedes the point.

"The problem is that the people working in marketing PR companies, the brand managers in big companies, *are* primarily middle-class south county Dublin. They don't know much about the GAA and what they do know is one of the guys they've heard of or seen in VIP," he says. "They want Seán Óg, or one of the Brogans, and they wouldn't know who Henry Shefflin is, or Eoin Kelly. They'd barely know who Joe Canning is. What that means is that they all end up chasing the same few players: if they had any sense they'd do what Underarmour did and pick off the up and coming fellas, the next generation of stars."

O'Keeffe points out that brands, PR and marketing people can be guilty of exploiting players: "They throw them into a picture, pay a few bob and then tend to walk away. Lucozade, in fairness, worked differently. They've had the Gooch and Henry Shefflin for a long time; they've built an association with them. Bord Gáis the same. They kept Joe Canning on board even when he moved out of the U21 grade that they sponsor, and people associate him with that company and that particular championship."

He also points out one very obvious issue for the GAA to tackle when it comes to promoting one of its main sports. Identification is tricky when you spend your career behind a face mask.

"Hurling has a problem," says O'Keeffe. "Tommy Walsh of Kilkenny wouldn't be known by people if he walked down O'Connell Street, but the rugby players and soccer players and Gaelic footballers don't have that problem.

"Can you quantify that? Of course you can. John Mullane, Dan Shanahan, Seán Óg—those are distinctive, identifiable fellas, but put helmets on them and they could be anybody. We had an issue with Vodafone last year. We did this whole outdoor shoot with Conal Keaney, but then we had to put a helmet on him. Sure it could have been me or you in the photographs. The GAA will have to bring in a rule where the players parade before championship games without the helmet, or are interviewed afterwards without them, because otherwise you're missing out."

O'Keeffe makes a lot of sense when he says that. The *Examiner* regularly runs a pre All-Ireland hurling final feature with head shots of the participants, inviting readers to identify them all. Few manage the full set. However, this is clearly blurring a line between a player endorsing a product for his own gain, and a player promoting a sport for the general good.

Given that the GAA is in competition with other sporting bodies for participation, however, should hurlers and footballers be compelled to promote their sports? Should GAA players be compelled to speak to the media, for instance?

——

"I've thought about this," says O'Keeffe. "Did Antonio Valencia want to go before the cameras when he got a vital goal for Man United in the Premiership? He's a guy with very little English having to face an interview in a language he's not that comfortable with. I doubt he wanted to, but contractually he was obliged to.

"I think the days of grey areas when it comes to the GAA and the media have to end, and the only way to do that is if county boards are compelled to put players forward. That's a payment issue as well, but you could have a series of graduated payments into a players' fund where, if you reached an All-Ireland semi-final, you could get €20,000 for the players' fund. But part of that would be players having to help promote the games, and engaging with the media to do that by, say, coming to a press day the week of the semi-final.

"Now that's a contractual issue, but in true GAA fashion we could probably fudge that somehow. My general answer is no, they shouldn't be compelled to promote the game, but we should come up with a system which regularises things. If Dublin, say, were told 'we'll get €20,000 for the players' fund if we get to a semi-final, but we'll have to produce a player or two for interview after every game', then I think they'd become available.

"The last ten years have shown that the more media-savvy the managers are, the better their teams tend to do. The worst-case scenario is what happened when Pillar (Paul Caffrey) had a media ban in Dublin, which created a pressure-cooker environment that didn't help the team, particularly."

Fair points, both about the advantages of being comfortable with the media when it comes to playing games and the potential of a financial reward system for the promotion of matches. But money and play are two words which tend to provoke a reaction when joined together in a GAA context.

Chapter 21 ∽

PEOPLE, AS THEY'RE ALSO KNOWN: THE GAA FAN AS CONSUMER

Everyone can recall their first trip to the revamped Croke Park, and the sheer event flash of being in a twenty-first century stadium which stunned its every visitor. The overseas press who attended rugby and soccer games in the venue were dutiful in their praise. A truly global event like the Special Olympics was the final endorsement, perhaps, if that were needed; final proof that here was a global stadium.

But nothing stays the same. From the new Croke Park Skyline tour you can see, if your knees haven't turned to jelly, the stadium's smaller but equally attractive counterpart across the Liffey, the Aviva. To compete and surpass the opposition, there's an onus on the GAA to impress and retain the consumer. Or to use Mick O'Keeffe's phrase: "People, as they're also known."

———

O'Keeffe puts the consumer challenge firmly in the GAA's inbox. "The big challenge now for the GAA is the recession, tightening up generally, emigration," says O'Keeffe. "In terms of marketing . . . From that perspective 2012 is the most competitive year for sport I've ever seen. Olympics, Paralympics, Formula One, Volvo Ocean Race, Euro 2012, rugby—and yet the GAA has a full suite of very good sponsors: Cadbury, Bord Gáis, AIB. It's done quite well given the sponsorship market—their share is about €10 million and that's pretty good. But what's more impressive is that the GAA is being more proactive— it's researching sponsors, it's looking for other ways to involve those sponsors, so you have SuperValu selling match tickets, for instance, and Diageo getting pouring rights in Croke Park.

"The argument was that ten years ago it was Guinness and Bank of Ireland organising all the press conferences, and the GAA was happy to go along with that, but as a result you had a situation where people weren't actually referring to a 'GAA' championship but to the Bank of Ireland championship, so the GAA wanted to take it back. If you remember it was the Guinness Hurling Championship—the posters in the pubs didn't even mention the GAA, for instance. Hence the multi-sponsor approach, which gives the GAA more ownership of the championships, and now everyone seems to be happy. Those are big brands in there. But a big challenge is offering value constantly."

———

This is relatively new ground for the GAA. The idea that you create an experience and offer value is, on one level, something that's anathema to a certain breed of GAA die-hard, someone who harks back to a time of 50,000 flat caps in the stands and terraces tracking the play. However, you can't put the genie back in the bottle. If people enjoy good service at another game, another sport, then they'll demand an equally good experience when they go to a GAA game.

O'Keeffe sees the GAA as working to offer that experience to punters nowadays.

"The GAA's staffed up, it's expanded its team and it's beginning to treat its consumers as consumers—or people, as they're also known— and the GAA is working hard to create entertainment. There's music, a fan zone and so on, and it's not quite there yet, but I think the All-Ireland semi-finals and finals last year had a real sense of occasion.

The Munster finals would have a different sense of occasion because they happen in a town, but they're working hard on creating a sense of occasion at big games in Croke Park. In fairness to the GAA, it was one sports organisation that saw the recession coming and worked hard—it's kept its prices down and offered great value. The Spring Series in Dublin is a good example—you can bring a kid for a fiver to see two games and a music group between those games."

There's also the GAA's ability to make a quick decision to cut prices: when the 2012 All-Ireland hurling final went to a replay, the Association dropped the top ticket cost from €80 to €50, which disarmed anyone accusing it of trying to cash in on the initial draw.

But despite the PR kudos, that cut still means a drop in funds coming in. O'Keeffe points out that an obvious stream of revenue for the GAA would be opening Croke Park again; after all, if you've done it once there's always the possibility of doing so again.

"Opening Croke Park was necessary. I'd say for many GAA people soccer rather than rugby was the problem, though rugby is probably more a threat to some GAA heartlands than soccer. I'd think there's an element of 'we need to stand on our own two feet and market our own product' to the decision, but I don't think the product is actually right.

"I'd like to think that Croke Park would be open and available for a Heineken Cup final in the future, though there are contracts in place with the Aviva that the FAI and the IRFU will never move to Croke Park—it's built into the Aviva contract—but that's more of an FAI/IRFU issue. But a Heineken Cup final would be different because it's ERC[European Cup]-related."

A repeat of May 2009 and Munster-Leinster again? Arguments can rage on over the relative strength of Munster in 2012 compared to their rivals, who put back to back European titles together while this book was being written, but even allowing for the downturn, that's the kind of one-off event that would surely fill Croke Park once again. And not just by Munster's traditionally strong travelling support either, as Mick O'Keeffe is keen to point out.

———

O'Keeffe says that while money is far tighter in the country, there are still "floating customers" available if they're courted properly.

"That's something the GAA has to embrace, the fact that the guy who's going to Donnybrook on a Friday can also head to Croke Park on Sunday—if you make it worth his while. I don't think 'rugby man' or 'GAA man' exists to the same degree. Those lines are breaking down.

"Take Limerick hurling. When they get on a roll they bring a huge crowd along with them. Munster rugby, Leinster rugby, those are huge bandwagons. You'd hear people who are close to the Leinster scene say that if the team went to the dogs they might have a core of 6,000 supporters; likewise, there are guys in Dublin who say if the footballers were in the horrors then the core support might be 12,000. That's the hard core. Both Leinster and Dublin need to expand their embrace, when you think of it."

What about the Dublin County Board's veiled attack on Leinster rugby, though? In late 2011 the Dublin Board's annual report referred to the capital's teams being of "monumental cultural and social importance to the city but, with over a fifth of the country's population resident here, they are also of enormous strategic importance to the future well-being of the GAA. While blue must become the colour of success, this is no cheap marketing gimmick."

Given the colour of the Leinster rugby jersey, it wasn't the most subtle flake across the knuckles. Dublin GAA wanted to mark their territory, which is understandable, but it's not an approach that's too conducive to O'Keeffe's dual embrace, as it were.

"I'd call myself a GAA man first and foremost," he says, "but the night of that announcement, I was MC at the Leinster rugby book launch, where Ciaran Whelan was guest of honour. I'd say Leinster rugby people were shocked. I thought it was unnecessary and showed a bit of insecurity.

"When you think of it, the seasons complement each other and there are companies who'd be interested in sponsoring both because the two of them cover a perfect cross-section of Dublin sporting society. Two teams in Dublin, both in blue, you sponsor those and you own the city, given the crossover in fan base and so on. Several of the

Dublin seniors played Cup rugby; Bryan Cullen works for Leinster. Sometimes I think the GAA would be better off concentrating on what it does best than paying attention to what's happening elsewhere."

Pointed comments like the Dublin County Board's "We can't copyright a colour but the subliminal exploitation of Dublin's unique sporting hue by our competitors has not gone unnoticed" aren't conducive to sponsors deciding to get Jonathan Sexton, Bernard Brogan and Liam Rushe down to a combined press call to push their product. An opportunity missed by Dublin? Looks like it at this point in time.

————

In any case there are in-house challenges which remain for the GAA. O'Keeffe sees room for improvement still.

"I still think we can make the customer experience better. We've done research on male and female dislikes in the area, and rugby registers off the scale when it comes to female popularity.

"It's a *very* female-friendly experience. The GAA is *quite* a female-friendly experience to come to, and soccer isn't particularly female-friendly. The facilities, the match-day experience could be made much better for the bandwagon fan, the occasion junkie. They exist, I know. They were looking for tickets for the Dublin-Kerry All-Ireland final last year (2011), people who'd normally be looking for Six Nations tickets."

Here's the poser for the GAA: do you want the bandwagon man who can pay top dollar for his tickets—the man who doesn't go to a GAA game from one end of the year to the next?

"Embrace the bandwagon. That'd be my motto," says O'Keeffe. "There can be a bit of 'what club are you from' when you're at a big game, and you shouldn't have to be from a GAA club to be at an inter-county game."

Why not? When it comes to recycling the ticket revenue throughout the Association, isn't the bandwagon man's money as good as anyone else's?

PART FIVE: INTERNAL CHALLENGES

Chapter 22 ∽

A DIFFERENT HYMN SHEET: WHEN THE GAA DISAGREES WITH ITSELF ABOUT MONEY

Into every life a little rain must fall . . . The GAA doesn't always get it right, of course. No organisation does.

We're not just talking about the occasional problem with money in clubs, though obviously that happens. In 2009 a Limerick GAA club treasurer was sentenced to a year in jail after huge holes were discovered in the club's finances. Eventually the person responsible had to sell a house in an effort to make partial restitution.

However, there are other financial problems which come up from time to time, challenges which take place in back rooms and outside committee meetings at the highest level within the GAA. For a glimpse of some of the power struggles over money within the Association, we spoke to a highly placed official who spoke plainly on condition of anonymity.

One issue he pointed to immediately was the GAA's insurance scheme, and the potential for friction between the provinces. This potential problem eventually ripened into actuality and the matter came to a head a couple of years ago between two provinces in particular.

"Essentially the GAA's player insurance scheme is designed to be self-funding and it's funded in a number of ways," said the official. "Every club is supposed to make a contribution as it registers teams, so your contribution depends on the number of teams you register as a club. You would also have contributions from the provincial councils along the lines of maybe six per cent of the gross gate receipts going to the scheme. Then you would have a contribution from Central Council as well.

"Right being right, then, whatever's paid in is drawn out, but looking at Munster as an entity, after we analysed it we found that Munster was contributing, over a three-year period, over €500,000 a year over what we were drawing out."

This would have been fine, obviously, if that money had been left in the kitty to offer a war chest for the following year's claims, for instance. Only that wasn't what was happening to the surplus. And the Munster Council wasn't happy with what was happening to the surplus.

"That extra money was being drawn out by other provinces. Over three years that oversubscription of €1.5 million from Munster, if you want to put it that way, was drawn out effectively by other provinces—Ulster, for instance, drew out €1 million more than it put in.

"We asked at that time whether people were getting more injuries in the north or whether people there were better able to utilise the system. What's been done since is that a club in any county, which is a net contributor to the scheme, is entitled to a rebate if that club registers on time. It's not an effort to discourage people from making a claim. That's not the point. It's more a way to stop people over-utilising the scheme, put it that way. Insurance is going up in all walks of life, but the benefits on offer from the scheme—which was under a lot of pressure a couple of years ago—are far better than anything on offer in other sports."

Then, of course, there was the obvious conclusion that could be drawn. Anybody with even a peripheral involvement with a GAA club will be aware of club-mates who might, for instance, be playing other sports to a high level yet who manage, somehow, to only pick up knocks and niggles while playing hurling or football . . .

"There was certainly a feeling at one stage that the GAA was taking the hit for injuries sustained playing other sports, though obviously any scheme of this nature is in line for that kind of thing," says the official. "There have also been claims made in clubs across the country, by the way, which have been queried, and action has been taken on a few of them—claims which were incorrect or inappropriate."

———

Beyond the insurance scheme, another issue which sometimes gets an airing is the division of TV and sponsorship revenue. More than once the argument has been made that in the interests of fairness and justice the relative strengths of the various provincial championships should be recognised with a proportionate allocation of funds; hence the widespread nervousness about the implications of the famous, or infamous, 'Champions League' format for the championship as a whole, as such an innovation would emasculate the provincial councils financially.

"If you look at it from a financial point of view," says our source, "in 2011 the amounts involved were €10.8 million in media income, and sponsorship was worth €8.1 million, and the total commercial revenue was €19 million. That's across the Association. Look at the media coverage. That comes predominantly from TV rights, and the All-Ireland final is the biggest draw of all. Munster has been arguing for an understanding of the valuation put on the Munster championships—from a commercial perspective and a TV rights perspective. The Munster Council would have seven games televised live and the media income would be €350,000 approximately.

"The argument could be made by Croke Park that more money goes back into the counties directly through grants and so on, but our view is that this isn't very clear. What happens is that this goes into what Croke Park calls the 'pot', but what we're looking for—as other councils are—is the maximum revenue we can disperse among the schools. That would also be a help to us, to put a commercial value on the championships.

"Let's be honest, there's a lot of talk about the Champions League structure, but to do that you'd have to make an informed decision. You can't do that without knowing the commercial implications if you go that route, and that's why we want greater clarity in terms of the commercial value."

There are specific reasons for wanting this clarity. The fact that Croke Park—as the GAA's headquarters, not the playing area—is based in Dublin, which is a vastly stronger economic area than anywhere else in Ireland, means that other large urban areas feel neglected.

"It would help to move the focus. It's great to have Dublin doing well, but we need to look at somewhere like Cork, which has a huge population and a GAA tradition, and we need to invest money there. Galway city is another black spot. We could have another six or seven coaches in Limerick city. That's another reason we'd like to know how the revenue is generated because while it's great that Dublin are doing well, they're able to generate money themselves."

This is a salient point and one that cropped up again and again in speaking to people—the fact that Dublin has more economic advantages as a city and county than any other area in Ireland. And the possibility is that that will begin to become more and more visible on the playing field in the seasons to come.

Chapter 23

PAYING FOR THE BISCUITS: THE COST OF GAA JUSTICE

It's fair to say the author has a dog in this fight, as they say.

In 2011 my club, Glen Rovers, played Bride Rovers in the Cork senior hurling championship. The game went to extra time, with the Glen eventually winning, but that's not why it was the subject of much discussion in the following days. A brawl occurred which involved many of the players and mentors, one which lasted longer than the usual brief confrontation to be seen in a hotly contested championship game, and retribution was swift.

The Cork County Board expelled Glen Rovers from the championship, and when the club appealed, though it was allowed back into the competition, there was a slight drawback when an incredible €10,000 fine was imposed. Or, as one member of the club pointed out, €2,500 more than the Dutch FA was fined for its team's shenanigans in the 2010 World Cup final.

Eventually the matter was resolved, after a great deal of huffing and puffing, not to mention the simultaneous release of oddly similar statements of apology from the two clubs—independent of each other, even more oddly. All's well that ends well. But the entire brouhaha does raise an interesting point.

What is the ethical basis for an amateur organisation imposing heavy financial fines on its clubs and county boards?

———

"If you look at it, the GAA's own constitution is all about the voluntary ethos and amateur ethos, so you'd wonder how that sits with it." The speaker is Jack Anderson, a lecturer in law in Queen's University Belfast. Anderson is very familiar with crime and punishment within the GAA, as he occasionally sits on the Association's disciplinary committees. He doesn't have an esoteric view of the philosophy of justice within the GAA; he has a far more pragmatic question about the effect of judicial decisions taken within the Association.

"My view from the disciplinary point of view is this—how effective is it? Particularly when you're dealing with county boards, what's happening is that they're centrally fined, so essentially what you're doing is recycling money with fines. The county board gives over money in a fine, but that money is then handed out again in grants. That seems completely ineffective, particularly when you add in the fact that the average inter-county player couldn't care less whether his county board is fined or not."

Anderson points out that the player is fined, not the county board, but clearly the county board pays the fine and not the player. Where's the disincentive there? Then there's the difference between clubs and county boards when it comes to the impact of a monetary fine. The former may have limited resources, but a hefty financial blow can bring a club to its knees.

"It's a kind of blunt justice," Anderson says, "and a bit of an easy way out, too. The fine is imposed and the money is paid out, but that money never leaves the GAA family, if you like. I don't know how effective that could be, obviously. The other side of it is that a fine imposed on a club will hurt that club, because it's not as big a unit as the county board. But in the case of Derrytresk GAA club, when a fine (of €5,000) was imposed for the brawl with Dromid Pearses in the All-Ireland junior football championship in Portlaoise, that fine was paid off by a local. You'd wonder if it'd be more fitting if that local was a builder, say, if he offered to build a new dressing-room instead of paying the fine.

"Overall, I think that other punishments could apply. You could go after players individually, or ban the club from competitions, but the fine itself seems a token gesture. That applies in professional sports, too, by the way. Last season in the Premiership, Manchester City were fined £30,000, which is meaningless for a club of that size and wealth."

Anderson also throws in a further consideration in GAA discipline. It's not uncommon to see the rules bend a little to facilitate a player's shot at the big-time: call it the 'semi-final dilemma'.

"It's all proportionate, and that should be the key to sanctions and punishments in all walks of life. It's understandable in a way with the GAA that there are so few competitions—many of them knock-out— that you have the 'semi-final dilemma'.

"A player does something in an All-Ireland semi-final which means technically that he should be banned, but he gets off for the final. Obviously if you ban a Premier League player for three games it's a drop in the ocean; he'll play in plenty more of them. But in the GAA the championship is everything to a player and there aren't that many games involved. Given the ineffectiveness of financial punishments, I think the GAA should consider more on-field bans. For instance, a sin bin would sort out a lot of nonsense—and would get rid of a lot of these appeals, too—because it'd be over in ten minutes, the player would calm down, and his team would be punished proportionately."

There's a further refinement Anderson offers. Strategic fouling is becoming more and more an issue in Gaelic football, in particular, and the legal expert points out a system that could be imported from another sport which would help on and off the field of play. "You could also have a system with a sin bin plus a 21 metre free, like basketball. Those would deal with a lot of the long-running appeals issues then afterwards because it'd be dealt with on the field and the vast majority of people would just get on with it afterwards."

Those long-running appeals processes are evidence of the GAA's system giving everyone another turn, says Anderson, but he points to horse racing as having a more efficient disciplinary system than, say, getting GAA players to sign a voluntary code of conduct in order to offset those never-ending appeals.

"Technically they do already (sign up) because they're bound by the rule book, though lawyers can argue that everybody has a constitutional right to the courts," says Anderson. "Symbolically it might be important to sign up to a code, but technically they do so already. The thing about the GAA's disciplinary system is that it always gives you another turn. There's an argument for a simpler system— one hearing and then one appeal and that's it. That works in racing, by the way: stewards look at an issue, there may be one quick hearing and then a final appeal, but that's it."

———

That's not how it happens in real life, of course. It's not uncommon to see a county board chairman engage in some sabre-rattling after an early-season red card for one of his county's players, pledging to exhaust every avenue to get justice for the man wronged by officialdom, but there's one small issue which the chairman will be well aware of. Justice costs money. Readers may remember the Semplegate fiasco of 2007, when the Cork and Clare hurlers had a bloodless tussle while taking the field for the Munster senior hurling championship.

Several suspensions resulted, with Cork—who had won the game and were therefore playing a Munster semi-final against Waterford soon afterwards—going through the entire appeals process in an eventually unsuccessful effort to free three of their players for that game. It was all good knockabout fun, with hilarious snippets emerging about the questions asked by some of the disciplinary committee men along the way, not to mention a last-gasp dash to Portlaoise on the weekend of the Waterford game. There was only one drawback for all concerned.

It cost thousands. One participant in the entire process was told that the bottom line figure, including all the traipsing up and down the country, left little change out of €25,000.

"That comes up now and again," says Anderson. "I sit on the Disputes Resolution Authority (DRA) panel the odd time, and you get mileage only. There was a hearing about the Monaghan footballers held in the Carrickdale Hotel and I claimed for a 90-mile journey, so it was €45 for the night. The DRA itself is quite inexpensive.

"It all depends on the parties involved. At the beginning with the DRA the parties always came in all lawyered up, though the GAA has done away with that to a large degree—it's usually represented by someone like Liam Keane of the DRA or Simon Moroney. Until lately Liam was the chair of the CHC (Central Hearings Committee) and Simon the CAC (Central Appeals Committee), and they represented the interests of both committees at the DRA hearing.

"Where it gets expensive is if a county brings in its own solicitor. Fergal Logan, the former Tyrone footballer, is a solicitor who represents a lot of northern counties and he does it for nothing, but many of them bring along a barrister as well, and he or she may charge for what is often a four to five-hour hearing. No doubt about that. In my view a good county board official would do as good a job as most lawyers, but many counties feel they need legal representation and they want to have it. However, if they lose, then the county is liable for costs. Then it starts to add up."

And when Anderson says it starts to add up, he's not kidding. Being liable for costs means springing for the pot of tea and the plate of chocolate biscuits provided for the DRA men, but that's the least of the losing side's worries.

"If you lose you'd have to pay for the costs of the arbitration itself, i.e. a €1,000 deposit, the hire of the hotel room for the evening, and the DRA panel's travel expenses. If Croke Park wins and the other side loses, then the usual rule is that the other side pays the winner's costs; the player or club will have to pay Croke Park's expenses as well, though they are not that costly.

"However, then there are your own expenses—travel and so on, paying the solicitor/barrister if you've brought one: some of them would be friends or members of a club, if it's a club that's involved, but a lot (some) aren't. It's business."

If it's a county board, then having a county team which is inclined to get its players sent off can become a costly business. Experienced GAA-watchers often detect the hidden hand of a county treasurer behind a senior team manager's public admission that his team will have to address a growing tendency to collect red cards.

"The cost of appealing disciplinary sanctions can add up if the team has a disciplinary problem, if lads are getting sent off and you're fighting all of those suspensions," says Anderson. "In fairness it's worth pointing out, though, that the alternative to that is getting a High Court injunction to prevent a game being played without player X or player Y, so the GAA's disciplinary system is still cost-effective.

"My only thing with it is you've to go to a hearings committee, an appeals committee and the DRA—that means three hoops, which is a system which could surely be simplified. In one way the fewer options people have, the fewer they're inclined to use, if you like. I remember sitting on the panel that dealt with Stephen Kernan's appeal when he was sent off playing for Crossmaglen. There was huge sympathy for him, but his argument was based on the fact that he was sent off on the linesman's advice, and that this was, technically, hearsay evidence only. Crossmaglen had a barrister there and may have had to pay for him, for the hire of the room in the hotel where the appeal was heard, and so on."

———

Leaving discipline to one side, are there other anomalies in the GAA rule book which are ripe for legal challenge—challenges with potentially costly repercussions for the Association as a whole?

"A lot of the matters before the DRA relate now to the parish rule and sometimes that undercurrent of alleged poaching of players by clubs, basically, with supposed coaching jobs and so on," says Anderson. "The European route is beyond the GAA, in general—European rulings on free movement and so on relate to professional sports people in their capacity as workers. With the GAA you have an amateur organisation working on traditional lines where there isn't as much of an economic effect.

"The only thing with the parish rule, mind you—and only in the North could they come up with this—is that while the rule book says the GAA is a non-sectarian organisation, obviously the parishes on which the parish rule is based are the parishes of the Roman Catholic Church, and you could ask 'what is a parish' in a modern civil society. The GAA's always trying to tighten its rules, but I'm living in Belfast and I don't think there is a parish rule, effectively, but I'd expect some kind of challenge to it down the line."

The ramifications for clubs of the removal of that rule would be enormous, particularly in urban areas with shared catchments. But Anderson points to other legal/economic oddities in the GAA world, like college students whose bursaries or scholarships are dependent on them playing for their particular institution.

"Are they *de facto* professionals? I suppose they are, in that sense. To all intents and purposes those college students are semi-professionals, but put it in a wider context. If you look at IRFU reports on club debts, those are huge. From growing up in Limerick I remember genuine senior rugby clubs that had three or four adult teams, but now they're barely surviving. The GAA could look at that: rugby is strong in Ireland in the sense that it has an international outlet and so on, but the IRFU can only sustain three and a half clubs."

That semi-professionalism is echoed in some managers' situations, says Anderson. "You may remember that when John Evans took over the Tipperary football team a few years ago, he was appointed director of football within the county to get around some rules about employment, and I think you'll get a bit more of that over the next few years.

"But generally, the payment of managers . . . everyone knows it goes on, but what can you do about that kind of 'car park payment' situation? I can see Páraic Duffy's point, that the manager should have vouched expenses like the physio or whatever, but the reality is that whatever happens outside that system, well, it's very hard to do anything about it, and people have said there are other things that the GAA could be focusing on. And in addition, it's up to managers themselves to make sure they're tax compliant, after all."

Anderson's parting shot is quite a cost-effective suggestion. His model is a sport that's usually cherished within the GAA for offering an international outlet, but he sees a far more practical template there than the gorblimeyed compromise that both organisations view as a sport.

"Economically the interesting thing for me is the AFL. It started in Melbourne, which has a population of four million, though obviously the country as a whole has 20 million inhabitants. But I saw that rugby league there recently signed a TV contract worth $1.2 billion—for a game that's only viable in parts of Sydney. The promotion of sport in Australia is unbelievable—and positive. It's not 'we're the AFL, we're not cricket'. The one thing that the GAA has learned, I think, is that you can't promote yourself negatively by saying 'we're not this and we're not that'.

"Generally I don't understand why the GAA doesn't have a full-time disciplinary officer. It relies on a lot of committees, and the more committees you have the wider the breadth of decision-making you'll meet. I think they could streamline that."

One man doing the job of three committees and taking one-tenth of the time those committees would need: surely nothing could be more economically viable than that.

Chapter 24 ∿

| LIKE A DIFFERENT COUNTRY

It was the kind of call any inter-county manager dreads: the last-minute venue switch. Jerry Wallace, Antrim hurling manager, was on the long road from his native Cork to Belfast when the Antrim County Board official rang with the bad news. Casement Park, where the county hurlers were due to train, was off limits for the evening. Instead, Antrim were going to have to hold that evening's session at an obscure club outside Belfast.

"I wasn't too happy," says Wallace. "I'd never heard of this place. From working with Cork and Limerick and handling club teams you'd always be wary of a venue switch like that. You'd be thinking to yourself, what kind of a spot are we going to end up in here."

When he got to the grounds, however, he was in for a surprise. The host club boasted three full-size pitches, one of them an all-weather surface, while its clubhouse is sleek and modern, with a lift—a lift!—connecting the floors.

"It was out of this world," recalls Wallace. "First-class facilities: we had a great session there. I came away thinking to myself, 'where the hell did this come from?'"

Given the polarising effects of the Troubles, not to mention the divisions between the two communities in the North during the relatively peaceful decades preceding the outbreak of violence, it's hardly surprising that one of those communities should row in wholeheartedly behind organisations which give it full cultural expression.

That doesn't explain the flowering of facilities in the GAA up north, however, described by one senior GAA official as "one of the great GAA stories". That's been funded by Britain.

––––

While this book was being written a brief storm blew up about sectarian sledging in a nondescript league game between Armagh and Laois. It all ended with a whimper as opposed to a bang, but during the imbroglio it was revealed that terms like "British bastard" were used; close observers of the scene can refer to past incidents when the "Queen's shilling" got an airing, with the intended insult that hurlers and footballers, presumably of a nationalist bent, would be insulted to pocket same.

Ironically enough, those throwing that insult around were a little closer to the truth than they may have realised; they just weren't expressing it properly. GAA director-general Páraic Duffy comes straight out with it when you raise the matter of top-class GAA facilities in the North.

"Ulster's been very successful in drawing down British Government funding. Look at the county grounds. Fermanagh—Brewster Park, a lovely ground; Armagh—new stand, wonderful; Newry, excellent ground; Omagh the same. Brand new stands with capacities of 15,000–18,000, plus the redevelopment of Casement."

The redevelopment of the main GAA venue in Belfast is a stunning success story for the Association in the Six Counties. There are already rumblings from traditionalists in Ulster about the possibility of moving the provincial final from Clones to Casement Park, but that's missing the story a little. The new facilities in Antrim are intended to be top of the range

"The British Government put up £110 million for the redevelopment of the three major sports stadiums in the North. Casement Park got £62 million, leaving £48 million for rugby and soccer combined. Fair play to them. A lot of the media down here wouldn't be aware of the huge progress that has been made in Ulster. People in the South have no idea of the quality of the clubhouses and facilities. What's happened up there is a great story."

Fair enough, but is that everyone's view? Leaving aside those already complaining that they don't want to leave Clones behind, there are more forcible objections being aired.

————

In Easter of 2012 Republican Sinn Féin attacked the GAA during the Party's commemoration at Milltown Cemetery. RSF Vice-President Geraldine Taylor said the GAA had "sold out its independence and the ideals of its founders when it accepted a massive amount of English money—£61 million—to develop Casement Park in Belfast. Roger Casement got the English hangman's rope, but those who use his name allow themselves to be exploited by Stormont, just as others contribute to the city of Derry—historic Doire Cholm Cille— being the British City of Culture in 2013. Those who pay the piper undoubtedly call the tune."

Speaking to the *Andersonstown News* later, Taylor expanded on that view: "Sinn Féin are using the good name of Roger Casement, who was hanged in an English jail, to accept blood money from England. They have forgotten our past. Where is the pride in that? Sinn Féin are well paid for what they are doing, yet our hospitals are in disarray, A&Es are closing and people are losing their homes. They are crying out for help and no one is helping them."

The reaction was swift. West Belfast Sinn Féin MLA Pat Sheehan dismissed it as nonsense. "The funding for Casement Park isn't some privilege or bribe. It is an entitlement that the GAA deserve. Irish cultural organisations have historically been underfunded. In fact it's fair to say that some have never received funding before. The fact that Sinn Féin sit on the Executive and the Assembly is ensuring that this balance is redressed. RSF's statement just shows the bankruptcy of the complete negativity that exists within the Party. What are they going to criticise next? Funding for Irish language groups? Irish medium education? The Gaeltacht Quarter?

"In contrast to their negativity, the GAA is a shining light within our communities. It would do them no harm to go around some of the clubs in west Belfast on a Saturday or Sunday morning to see the leadership that the GAA provides to our young people. They are making facilities available for our young people to develop them and provide them with friendships . . . No one wants them (RSF); no one wants to listen to their message. It's an absolute nonsense and they have nothing positive to offer—in contrast to the GAA."

———

For anyone who grew up in the seventies or eighties the GAA's place in the new Northern Ireland takes a little getting used to. A random trawl of news stories will throw up gems such as the recent praise for the Association from the Northern Ireland Justice Minister, David Ford, who lauded the GAA for its continued commitment to community engagement and a shared future at a meeting with GAA officials at the provincial headquarters in Armagh.

Ford said: "A key priority for my Department and the Executive is a shared future for all. It is clear that the GAA has a similar vision through its programmes of work, which complement that of my Department on a shared future strategy." Very impressive indeed, and of a piece with the British Government's decision to fork over vast amounts of money.

You dig a little deeper, however, and you learn why exactly this happened: it's because the GAA in Ulster threatened them with the law. In 2005 the Ulster Council secretary Danny Murphy threatened to sue the Department of Culture, Arts and Leisure for inequality of funding.

Rather than going to court, the British Government decided to pony up. Since then the GAA has received an estimated €120m in public money. Journalist Paddy Heaney has made the salient point that the GAA's contribution to the redevelopment of Casement Park, a once-off contribution of £15 million, is dwarfed by that of the British Government. The argument could be made that the GAA is getting a state-of-the-art new stadium for just that: £15 million.

The most obvious comparison is with other infrastructural projects, such as Pairc Uí Chaoimh in Cork, which has been variously and conservatively estimated at €40 million. Unfortunately for officials in the southern capital, there's nobody around that can be threatened with a lawsuit which might lead to a cash subvention; hence the nervousness among club secretaries all over the Rebel County as they await a letter from the Cork County Board asking them to raise funds for a project that goes over budget.

The less obvious comparison is with government funding of the GAA in Ireland: the lottery. We'll come to that soon enough.

Chapter 25 ⌁

PAYING FOR FAILURE: MANAGERS

The exact identities need not detain us, nor those of their respective lawyers, but suffice to say the two men involved were well known. One was an inter-county forward with a superb goal-scoring record, the other a coach without superb man-management skills, and their relationship had never been that close.

Eventually an exchange at training one evening summed up the distance between them.

The player had been offered a decent endorsement gig in the capital, a handy €1,000 for one day's work, and as a consequence he was informing the manager that he'd be unavailable the following Thursday.

"That doesn't work for me," said the manager, shaking his head. "I need you to be at training that evening."

"I'm not going to be there," said the player. "That's a lot of money to me: it'll pay for a holiday for me, the wife and the kids after the season ends, a 'thank you' to herself for minding them all summer."

"Look," said the manager. "You're going to have to give it a miss. I need everyone here on Thursday, and if you're not around you won't be playing in the championship because you won't be ready."

The player missed his payday, and later he worked the dialogue into a neat set-piece story, with much accurate impersonation of his manager and a fine pay-off line to finish. "I wouldn't mind so much," the player would say, "but he [the manager] left training that evening and went out and hopped into a car that the county board were paying for. And I missed out!"

———

It's more than a funny story, though. The exchange shows the inherent tension that exists between a manager who's being paid and amateur players who may be out of pocket, missing overtime, extra shifts or promotion opportunities, or simply not seeing their family by virtue of their membership of an inter-county panel.

The whole manager payment issue took on a life of its own early in 2012 with a good deal of huffing and puffing about the matter, and about what needed to be done, when in truth there wasn't much that could be done.

Then-GAA president Christy Cooney didn't win many friends when he pointed out that people had a personal responsibility to ensure they were tax-compliant, but he was correct. Pundits and the public felt that county boards should not be facilitating these under-the-counter payments, but the reality is that county boards don't pay managers. As one former inter-county manager remarked to me, if you wanted to catch managers being paid you'd have to trawl through hotel car parks and motorway service stations to see the various backers and boosters, the businessmen and tycoons who are paying these managers.

This was neatly illustrated when, in March 2012, former Dublin manager Tommy Lyons suggested he'd been offered payment by a county. "When I was there and I was interviewed for the job," Lyons said at the time, "I was asked to put it in an envelope what I wanted to get paid for doing the job and I asked him what part of 'I don't want to get paid' did he not understand? So that was a senior inter-county official as of only 12 months ago in a very clear breach of the guidelines."

Lyons didn't name the county at the time, but the Mayo County Board wasn't long in denying that it was the county board in question ("Payment was never discussed," said the board PRO. "Mileage was, however, talked about as we tried to ascertain whether Tommy would be travelling from Dublin or from his holiday home in County Mayo, where he spends a lot of time.")

Fair enough. But then the county board official went on to reinforce the point made above: "That's not to say that somebody outside of a county board officer didn't approach Tommy Lyons with an offer of payment for his services, but at no time was Tommy Lyons offered payment by a county board officer."

We didn't do it, but we don't know if someone else did it, so don't be giving out to us if the manager in question suddenly drives a current year registration car, ok? It was nothing to do with us.

———

Having been a selector with a county team which won an All-Ireland, Eamon O'Shea can offer the perspective of someone who's aware of the incongruities involved.

"When we were involved with Tipperary none of us was paid and I wouldn't be comfortable being paid even if, sitting around the table with me, there were people who were being paid. In our management team myself, (manager) Liam Sheedy and (selector) Michael Ryan were not being paid. But if I went to another county I wouldn't have a problem being paid for that for the hassle it causes me, though I wouldn't be interested in being paid for working with a club team. I'm not dogmatic about it."

O'Shea also points out that there's an odd side-effect arising from payments to managers: a lot of them are being paid for failure.

"The payment of managers is interesting because the viability of paying managers asks serious questions about the *selection* of managers. That's largely a matter of the prospective manager's iconic image: the higher up on the icon index, the higher the guy's chances of getting a job, but nobody asks if the guy can manage or coach. If you get into that it raises interesting issues. There's a finite talent base, so the same names are always being touted for managerial vacancies, but in addition, fellas are being paid for failure—for failing every year. Nobody seems to point that out."

Moreover, as with many economic situations within the GAA, the paid-manager issue comes in two sizes. The county board which chooses to bring in a hired gun can be viewed as having more money than sense, and if it wishes to waste that money on a manager who may not improve their teams, fine: it's a situation a lot of GAA members would find distasteful, but it's a matter for the county board in question. However, the club which takes that step has far fewer resources, by definition. And as O'Shea points out, while a county board can carry the can for physiotherapists, psychiatrists, masseurs and nutritionists, most clubs can't. As befits a professor of economics, the Tipperary man takes a dispassionate view of how clubs go about selecting managers.

"The typical GAA club loses all sense of rationality when it comes to picking a manager for the top team in the club," he says. "Now maybe it's expediency—'your man was with such and such last year and they did ok', yeah. No one asks if such and such won, or whether they won crucial games, or how they played, or whether the way they played will suit the new club. It's interesting that some people are being paid at the moment, and what is happening is that you're paying people for failure. And clubs don't have that money, and I think it's wrong.

"If I ever went to a club I wouldn't take money from them because they don't have the resources. They should be developing their own management and coaching structures—it's an indictment of the club not to have that. Now it's fair enough to seek advice, to ask someone how training should be organised, or whether the team should be training four nights a week in January or whatever. That's fair enough.

"But that brings us to another point. The payment issue is skewing the preparation and training of teams. It is skewing preparation towards particular ways of training teams and it is biasing training regimes."

So you have the perfect vicious circle. Given the communication between inter-county players via text, via Twitter, via Facebook, the exact nature of training regimes in one county is circulated in other counties. County X has a sports psychologist who comes in to talk to the panel once a week; a player with County Y finds this out via Facebook and asks his manager why they don't have a sports psychologist coming in once a week—or better, twice a week. Is the net result, then, a series of costly regimes which must be matched euro for euro?

"Exactly. That's not just an economic issue, by the way. It goes to everything. I find now that when I was coaching in NUI Galway that you'd come in and the players would practically fold their arms, with an expression of 'I bet you can't come up with a drill I haven't seen before—impress me.' I felt you'd have to say, 'Listen, I don't have to impress you, man. You've got to impress me. I'm the guy who puts your name down on the team-sheet'.

"Then it gets worse because you have useless derivatives of drills, complex hand-passing drills, for instance, that you'd wonder, 'when is the player going to have to use that skill?' When is he going to have to give a reverse hand-pass over his shoulder while on his knees, for instance, when in actuality a player has to strike the ball every ten seconds?"

How much of this—the shadow economy of failing coaches, the consequent blizzard of bizarre drills aimed at 'challenging' players—is down to the lack of a serious coaching career infrastructure? Coaching as a job with prospects of progression in the GAA has always seemed a pretty *ad hoc* proposition.

"Well, it goes back to the payment of managers in a way, because I think you have to have qualified managers," says O'Shea, "qualifications to coach, to organise. If I were coaching Tipperary properly, for instance, then there should be a hurling committee which dictates policy, and that policy filters down to the U21s, minors, U16s, U14s. I don't need to coach those teams but I'm responsible, in that scenario, for the organisational structure, for hiring those coaches because I've been hired on a five-year contract or whatever.

"A by-product of the lack of coaching structures is that there's a lot of derivative coaching going on, and we should really up the ante there in terms of standards, and what matters and what doesn't matter. I think standards are being diminished because of *ad hoc* payment structures, poor wages, poor promotion structures. They end up working in areas for a couple of years and then they're gone. What you need is consistency.

"What happens as a result? You can have the wrong people coaching young lads. I'm not saying they shouldn't be involved, but they may not have the technical expertise needed, so young lads' skills are not properly developed or they're concentrating on the wrong skills, and there's nobody there to take an overall view."

That doesn't necessarily have to be confined to the county level either, adds O'Shea. Each club could have a person whose responsibilities would revolve around the playing style of that club: "There should be someone in every club to say, 'This is the way we need to teach our young lads to develop. We need to develop these aspects of our game.' But instead clubs are focused solely on the senior hurling team, and by the time players get there, it's over. No matter if Brian Cody is managing them by that time, they're not going to progress."

―――

Enda McGuane acknowledges O'Shea's point, and he and his colleagues have moved to address the career path problem.

"We're working on something like that: Joey Carton is working on a document for us, on taking guys at club level and educating them not so much in coaching but in managing a team in the holistic sense. We're hoping that that will educate people in what to look for, in what pitfalls to avoid, in what's actually required taking on a coach, rather than just getting in a big name."

McGuane has a specific interest in fiscal responsibility on the part of GAA clubs, and it isn't one that relates to improving the striking skills of ten-year olds from Clare to Waterford: proper financial management in clubs might just help with his insomnia.

"You were asking about what keeps me awake at night in terms of fears for the GAA and so on," he says. "Well, that's it. I see club accounts all the time. I see the amount of expenditure from small junior and intermediate clubs on managers, and you'd have to ask, 'What benefit did you get from that? Are there young lads developed; is the team any better?' It's all about the pursuit of success, but there's always only one winner. There aren't any short cuts, which is something a lot of these clubs have to learn.

"For instance, Kilkenny win All-Irelands because they have a great team, a great manager. But when they weren't successful back in the nineties they carried out a root-and-branch examination of where they were; they got former players who felt they could make a contribution involved at underage level; and they developed very strong structures as a result. But it didn't happen overnight, and we've lost sight of that, particularly at club level."

There's a recognisable and often-repeated scenario that McGuane deals with on a regular basis. "What can happen is that a new chairman of the club gets elected at the AGM; he decides they'll win the championship they're involved in, whether that's junior, intermediate or senior, no matter what it costs. He spends the money and then is gone three years later, and a new chairman and executive is left with a club in a lot of debt. That's what we're dealing with. And that's what we're trying to avoid in the future."

There's another downside to the paid manager, but it's not financial—at least, not obviously.

Chapter 26 ∿

FIXTURE MIGRAINES: THE INFLUENCE OF THE OUTSIDE MANAGER

There's another side to the great evil of the outside manager, as mentioned in the last chapter, but it's one that doesn't get mentioned too often.

No, it's nothing to do with his ability to corrode the very fabric of the Association by filling his pockets thanks to the takings from a little club's bingo night etc. At county level the manager has a little-known power, an ancillary power that goes along with that day-glo *Bainisteoir* bib that few people remark upon. It's at once more banal and yet potentially more damaging to the county board than simple avarice. It's his power over fixtures.

———

Christy Cooney is a non-believer when it comes to the cult of the outside manager. One of the corner-stones of his argument against the concept is the undue power they wield in some cases.

"Managers who come in from the outside, some of them getting paid, get a lot of scope. That doesn't traditionally happen in counties with a tradition of success. I believe in home-grown managers because it's part of you, it's in your heart. That's not to say an outside manager won't bring that, but he's gone after three years. You want to bring a structure, to have a continuum within the county. A local manager knows the club structure, knows what's expected—the Corks, Kerrys, Tipperarys, Kilkennys, for instance, are used to doing that."

Cooney's point is valid. The new outside manager knows the clock is ticking from the moment he's unveiled, though there's rarely a formal event heralding his arrival. (Incidentally, GAA reporters often remark that it seems odd that a new outside manager who is probably costing his new county board thousands is almost never presented professionally to the media and public. You'd imagine a high-profile arrival who is nominally on hand to boost the county's profile as well as improving performances on the field would be worth even a perfunctory press call, but it hardly ever happens.)

Cooney goes on to suggest the demand for results means the outside manager is under "greater pressure" for wins, and that can have a knock-on effect when it comes to fixtures within the county because the new boss wants his inter-county players to himself. County board officers charged with running that side of operations can be compromised.

"Bringing in an outside manager—he's brought in to be successful, so he's under greater pressure, so he's going to demand a lot of time with the players," says Cooney. "People must realise that no team is a manager's team. It's the county team, the clubs' team. They're on loan from the clubs to the county. There must be balance. Of course county players need time together, but you must have balance. That's the big challenge for a county chairman or secretary.

"A new manager shouldn't be under any illusions about the championship structure of the county he's come to, and people within that county must also be realistic about what can actually be achieved. Expectations must be realistic—counties training in the close season . . . players killing themselves in October because their manager feels he has to achieve. And that's unfair to the manager, too."

If you feel that the odd fixture pile-up is nothing to worry about, consider this. A county where club players may be idle for months between championship games is one where those club players lose interest and drift away, reducing competitiveness; it's one which shoehorns its championship into the start and the end of summer, which shows administrative inefficiency; it's a county which can be ridiculed for wasting money on an unsuccessful manager who has wreaked havoc on fixtures within the county—all in, not an attractive prospect for a county looking for commercial sponsors.

———

At the end of the day, though, surely manager payments is an issue between the manager, his conscience and the Revenue Commissioners? Cooney prefers to focus on the failure of a county to produce an indigenous manager.

"There's a bigger issue (than the manager's conscience), which goes back to county boards appointing a manager, and the conditions agreed between the board and the manager at that time.

"I'd question anyone who'd say there's nobody within a particular county to manage that county's team. It comes back to good coaching structures in a county. You hear people say someone is able to coach an U16 team but not a senior team, though the U16s may be more difficult to handle with all their physical and mental development, school and so on. It's ego you must manage at senior level. They can all play. There are capable people in every county and it's down to players to work with them.

"The manager must be strong enough to run the show, and it's certainly not always the manager who's to blame if the team fails. There's a respect element. The person's been appointed because he's the best man for the job, and he deserves respect. I've no problem with former players getting involved with a county board to find a manager, but at base I believe in the home-grown manager. Money should never be the issue. As chairman in Cork no manager I was involved with—Jimmy Barry-Murphy, Larry Tompkins, Billy Morgan—money was never a factor. They were driven to be successful for the county, for the players, and if there was a bonus for them, great. But there are people like that in every county. Anyone who gets involved in the GAA for money is in cloud cuckoo land, anyway. That's not what it's built on. That's not the remit."

———

Cooney is inclined to see a change in attitude when it comes to money and management, at both club and county level. There may be less money sloshing around for under-the-counter payments anyway, but on-field performances may be even more persuasive than the recession.

"Is that [club manager payments] more pernicious than inter-county managers getting paid?" says Cooney. "I think it's a question of clubs copying what they see at inter-county level, but soon I think there'll be a proposal which will move the inter-county management issue forward. But having said that, I think there's a realisation at county level that money doesn't win championships, that outside managers aren't necessarily a solution, and that they need to manage their books in a better way. That's certainly recognised by the GPA, that money isn't the be-all and end-all, that it's about structures, hard work, and being honest. I think players are wise enough to realise 'we can't have everything we used to have. It's a different world now; we have to move forward.'"

Enda McGuane also takes the view that mindless copying of other teams has led to problems—take the explosion of the backroom team in particular. "We hear this nonsense about teams training at half five in the morning and then going off to work. I did that, and did it in the Army as well, and the benefits of doing that, or doing 30 sessions on the trot, are that it bonds the group, supposedly. The physical benefits are fairly questionable, I think.

"The point was made recently about just how many people were involved in inter-county teams who *shouldn't* be involved with those teams. There are attempts to professionalise the set-up, one of which is having as many people involved in the set-up as possible.

"But if you look at everything from a business perspective, if you have skill level X within a county team, what do you need to improve that? It's not a question of what another county is doing, or just having the bodies around. In the latter case you have to ask what those people are doing to make the team better. That's what needs to be asked."

Look inside the county to improve how you'll perform outside, rather than ape what's going on elsewhere. Cost-efficient on all levels.

Chapter 27 ∿

WHEN CHAMPIONSHIP RESTRUCTURING CEASES TO BE A CONVERSATION KILLER

You could call it conversational Kryptonite. Wherever two or three GAA supporters gather together and start chatting about Henry's injury or Mickey Harte's squad, there's always one way to bring the talk to a screeching halt, one killer question that stubs out conversation like a lit fag landing in a puddle. "Well lads, what would ye do to restructure the championship?"

You've probably feigned death yourself at some point to avoid talking Champions League/provincial series abolition/groups of four, eleven, eight, ten. And that's a pity, because as the GPA, marketing men and ex-presidents of the GAA point out in this book, a properly structured championship would serve players, the GAA, the public and—significantly—the GAA's accountants very well.

Try to stay awake.

———

With the air of a man accustomed to talking to teenagers who operate off a low boredom threshold, John Considine takes the plunge.

"There's no point advocating it because it wouldn't have a snowball's chance in hell of being adopted, though I don't mind being associated with it," he says in a less than ringing endorsement of his own views.

"But you could cut the inter-county season in hurling to six weeks. When I played, the league was viewed as a preparation for the championship. Now the Waterford Crystal and Walsh Cup are viewed as preparation for the league, and managers are talking about burn-out so they can prepare for those early-season tournaments—tournaments that are preparation for the league, which are in turn preparation for the championship.

"But you can play a Rugby World Cup in six weeks. You could take the 12 teams in the MacCarthy Cup to play off in three groups of four and get semi-finalists and finalists, no problem. The football could be run off in eight weeks."

However, this is where reality bites. It would benefit the clubs and the players, but the pain would be too severe for accountants to handle, he thinks.

"The thing is you wouldn't generate funding," says Considine. "You'd lose TV coverage and you'd go back to the days of very few matches on TV, though it would free up time for the club game. You wouldn't have a hope, though, because it would cost the Association. It would cost the Munster and Leinster Councils, for instance, who would instantly oppose a move like that.

"Commercially the GAA is aware of that. It spaces out games, and the model that's working now works quite well because they keep so many people from being unhappy, put it that way. There are so many people being pulled and dragged everywhere, but the system maintains a kind of low-level peace.

"But look at it another way when it comes to coverage. How often do you see Henry Shefflin on the television, one of the best players we've ever seen? Take his counterparts in rugby, you'll see the players at provincial level, never mind national level, on a very regular basis. That's another aspect to this. A few years ago Limerick played Offaly in the hurling qualifiers and there were 7,000 at it—but 100,000 watched it on television. That's a significant viewing figure for an event with a very small crowd physically present for it."

Considine makes a significant point which you can expand into an interrogation of attitudes, if you like: do you consider yourself a GAA follower if you make a point of tuning in for a game like GAA-Limerick, no interruptions and all your supplies to hand on the couch? Do you consider yourself a GAA follower if you wouldn't spare a flick of the remote for that game but would prefer to head out to watch your own club's U15s?

––––

When Considine says the current system is one that keeps "so many people from being unhappy", it's an accurate description. The back-door system increased the number of games and gave players a second chance, having operated for decades under a system which gave half the participants one game, possibly two, after six months' training.

But many people now believe the inter-county season is too long. Not the GAA season, because obviously that varies from county to county, but the inter-county season—given the small numbers involved directly—tends to act as a tail that wags the dog, throwing fixture plans everywhere into chaos. One of those who feels the inter-county season needs shearing is former GAA president Christy Cooney.

"At Convention I've advocated a championship structure of four eights (four eight-team groups) and I think that'll happen in time. John Prenty of Connacht (Council) advocated something similar recently. The championship season is too long. It's too drawn out. I believe we need to balance the structure of the provincial championships to give more teams a chance to compete.

"We're talking in May, yet you could name the half-dozen teams with a chance of winning the All-Ireland now—in hurling and football alike. We need to give other teams a better chance of competing, to get through more championship rounds. An eight-team structure would help there."

Cooney admits, though, that administrators at county level would need to hold the line with scheduling to make that work: "I think we can tighten it up, but county boards need to be strong enough to give a proper championship structure, then, for their clubs. "There's no point in making that change only to have an inter-county manager come in then and say, 'I need the players for five or six weeks.' One thing won't happen without affecting the other."

Mick O'Keeffe offers a little context for the championship restructuring ideas: he points out that they can't be divorced from the GAA's commercial outlook as a whole. Which isn't to say he doesn't have a particular structure he favours. Of course he does . . . "From a GAA perspective generally, commercial models are difficult," says O'Keeffe. "We hear companies say, 'oh, the GAA should be more like Leinster Rugby' or whatever. But it's not. It's very different. From a GAA perspective there probably is a lot more money that could be made, and you'd have to say the Yanks are years ahead of us when it comes to things like pre-game entertainment and so on.

"But they have a different outlook on sport—they can see it as entertainment, whereas the GAA is something more deep-rooted and traditional, and you could say the same about sport in England.

"However, you can only go so far with that, and as long as the GAA runs its championships on an antiquated provincial system, and doesn't bear marketing and promotion of the games in mind, then we're going to be in trouble. People say to me, 'well what would you do to promote the championships better', and I always give the same answer. You can't start promoting the championships until you improve how they're run in the first place. You have a system where Galway can play a first-round game and then have no game for nine weeks. You have a Connacht championship that begins in May—in New York—and doesn't end for 12 weeks."

The clash of commerce and tradition jars with O'Keeffe, who has a particular—and long-standing—animus against the beginning of the GAA inter-county championship in particular.

"That makes no sense at all. The GAA can't be commercially minded and then run it on an antiquated system. The championship begins with a whimper—Donegal-Antrim in a horror show in Ballybofey, or Roscommon-New York on an artificial pitch. You can't fool the consumer any more. Dublin supporters know if they lose to Kildare they're still in the championship; so do Cork if they lose in Killarney.

The championship begins in August. We've discussed here in the office the possibility of rebranding or relaunching the championship come August—the same way they have a Big Four weekend or March Madness in the States."

And structure? "I'd try eight groups of four," he says. "And a 'Super Saturday', four big games on a Saturday night, four on a Sunday. The TV lads could plan it out in advance. The clubs would benefit because they'd know where players are going to be. It'd be a proper tournament."

——

One last thing. Though TV stations could plan their broadcasts and supporters would be able to rely on a set number of games, isn't there one drawback? Don't bigger, richer teams inevitably dominate league-style tournaments? You look around the world at professional sports leagues and despite the odd eulogy to the likes of the Oakland A's in baseball thanks to 'Moneyball' (a team, remember, which was more competitive but still unsuccessful), Voltaire called it right all those years ago when he almost said God is on the side of the big battalions.

"Say you have two teams playing and one team has roughly a 30 per cent chance of winning," says Considine. "In other words, if they played ten times it'd win three of those games. If that goes to the best of three games then that team's percentage goes down to 21.6 per cent. Therefore if you go over to the league system totally it's dominated by the bigger, better teams. The back-door system in the championship, for instance, has added an extra round to the championship, but it could also be argued that it cost Waterford or Wexford the 2004 All-Ireland hurling championship. The question is this—what do you want?"

At last somebody asks the basic question that all championship restructuring debates need to ask: what's the objective? Everyone is pretty clear on what they don't want from championship structuring, but like those who oppose the bail-out and austerity, realistic alternatives are few and far between.

"Do you want to balance things out?" adds Considine. "We think knock-out is great for that, but imagine an All-Ireland championship draw which was structured with all the strong teams on one side and the weaker sides on the other. You could have Kilkenny and Tipperary playing each other in the first round, with one being eliminated, and Laois making it to the All-Ireland final from the other side of the draw.

"That would be great for the development of hurling in Laois, but there wouldn't be as big a demand for tickets for the All-Ireland final. Or too many people wanting to watch it on television. There's a constant tension between relative competition and absolute competition, and that happens in other sports too. If it didn't you wouldn't have a home quarter-final as a reward for winning your Champions League group stage."

If TV audiences dropped in such a scenario, what would happen match attendances? It's fair to presume that crowds wouldn't hold up too well, if the evidence from other competitions in Ireland is anything to go by. Considine doesn't look too far for an example of a sport which had huge attendances within the last 40 years, but which collapsed totally and has yet to recover.

"Look at the League of Ireland. People laugh at that league and the attendance figures, but think about it. If the Cork senior hurlers and footballers played the same number of games, on a league basis, that Cork City FC play, how many would you get on average? If you had a Gaelic football inter-county league with 15 teams, on average how many would the Cork footballers attract? Two thousand? You're in League of Ireland territory there, and while people laugh at those attendances, how different are they really from GAA league games? When people talk about the popularity, they're back to the championship, not the league. Why? Because they prefer knock-out. And that's popular in soccer, too. Don't forget the Champions League has a knock-out element. It's not just a league. People calling for change seem to forget that aspect of it."

Footfall, TV viewing figures. The Champions League's resemblance to the Championship. Who knew championship restructuring could actually be interesting?

Chapter 28 ◡

THE EXPENSE OF ECUMENISM, OR WHY ONE-CODE COUNTIES DO BETTER

Here's an obvious one: how much easier is it to succeed if your county focuses on one code, when you can use the word 'cheaper' instead of 'easier'?

Looking at the record books, there's only one answer. The most successful county in Gaelic football is Kerry, which has only a pocket of hurling in one corner to the north but has collected 36 All-Ireland football titles. In hurling there's Kilkenny, 34 senior titles and no Gaelic football of any description to judge by some of the hammerings handed out early in 2012 at all grades: they conceded 6-34 to the Louth U21s, for instance.

Former GAA president Seán Kelly—and Kerryman—doesn't beat around the bush when you ask whether it's a huge economic advantage to have just the one elite code to concentrate on.

"Without a doubt in the world," he says without hesitation. "It's one of the things I'd have often thought about, the dual mandate in counties. The more I see of the success of Kerry and Kilkenny, the more I'd despair for other counties and their chances of making a breakthrough. I'd be thinking of the likes of Westmeath, Carlow, Roscommon—counties trying to apply themselves in both codes, and as a result of that they're never going to be good enough at either. They don't have the resources, particularly in terms of manpower, to succeed, and players won't be committed to one sport rather than the other. It's much easier to succeed if you focus on one code over the other."

The standard bearers for the dual mandate have to recognise that reality, says Kelly. "Even a big county like Cork can see that; the likes of Eoin Cadogan, lads doing both sports, are few and far between. It's getting more and more difficult. I've changed my mind on this, actually. Going back the years to the likes of Ray Cummins and these players, I thought it could still happen in the modern game. But I'm beginning to change my mind. It's a pity, but if your aim is to be successful, then you need to concentrate on one code."

It's not just a matter of accommodating players; it's an issue of finite resources as well. "When you're successful it's easier to promote the game, obviously. I can see that for myself in Kerry, where you get a great boost when you win an All-Ireland. I'd ask myself then, though, 'how do they keep it going in counties where they don't have any success?' I suppose in some respects they're keeping it going, just at another level. To close that gap would take a huge effort. And huge resources."

―――

Another former GAA president can articulate the Kilkenny position with more credibility than most. Nickey Brennan played in the Leinster senior football championship for Kilkenny in 1982, the year the Cats won the All-Ireland in hurling. When he says he has a grá for football, he can prove it.

"First, there's no economic issue with Kilkenny football," says Brennan. "What's played in the club scene in Kilkenny is social football. My own club would play more football than most, and would train early in the year, but the football is left to one side as the hurling warms up. But we have to accept that that's the level, the social aspect, though earlier this year I quoted a statistic in an article for the *Kilkenny People*—in March or April there'd been 120 games of football played in the county. I pointed out that at inter-county level we stood indicted, but at club level we played a lot of games at all levels, leaving standards to one side. You could compare that figure to the hurling games played in a lot of counties. Admittedly, there's a downside—about 50 games had been given as walk-overs. That's the negative. But there are a lot of games played."

Yet the reality is that Kilkenny can then focus all their efforts on hurling, unlike other counties making a realistic attempt at both codes. Some of those dual counties might have taken grim satisfaction in the GAA's decision to send the Cats to play football in England for 2013; for one thing it means the Kilkenny County Board will have to put some serious money into the big ball.

"The county board's made a decent effort working on this, though we probably need to be more radical," says Brennan. "I don't know what to make of this playing in England idea. Well done to whoever came up with it, but unless we give it a go then it'll just be a one-year wonder. And this is where economics really comes into the equation. Bringing people over to England . . . I met a Waterford County Board official recently who'd have accompanied Waterford teams to England on games, and he pointed out that bringing a group of 30 people to England would leave you little change out of €15,000. Multiply that by four and it's sixty grand. I'd imagine Croke Park or the Leinster Council would come in and fund half of the costs, maybe. Is it a long-term solution? I don't know."

The reaction to those 2012 defeats was a little hysterical in places, some commentators calling for punishment for the Cats for somehow bringing the game into disrepute. Was that unfair?

"I don't know if I'd use the word 'unfair'," says Brennan. "They were awful hammerings, and most of them happened at underage level, but the seniors were well beaten too. It's not nice to see. I was at the Fermanagh and Wicklow games and they didn't make for great viewing. Ultimately it was down to players who weren't fit enough, who weren't coached—they were fish out of water. You might ask, then, why do they bother, but there's a cohort of people in Kilkenny, players and supporters, who have a genuine interest in the game. You have to make up your mind what you want when it comes to the

GAA—when you get involved you buy into a number of things. You buy into the games, into the culture. How much is a county going to do to support those? When it comes to one game we're way up on top. With the other game we're off the radar. That's the reality. You can't ram anything down a person's neck, but in all honesty Kilkenny football is on life support and God knows if it's going to get better or not. We may be getting to the stage—which I hope we aren't—where that life support will have to be turned off and that's it. And it may have to be resurrected in another form in a few years' time."

The Kilkenny man sees the clubs as bearing the brunt of the responsibility: "The whole thing is down to apathy from the clubs. Some of the players representing Kilkenny in recent games have been probably third choice, and that's not being disrespectful. If you had the very best of what's available—forget about hurlers, you don't want hurlers—in terms of athletes, put them on a good winter programme, then Kilkenny football would be respectable in Division Four. And only respectable in Division Four.

"But if the English experiment doesn't work, then the thing will be dead in the water and Kilkenny will be gone from the inter-county scene."

Chapter 29 ❧

| THE PAID OFFICIAL

Then there are the little storms that nobody sees coming. The GAA isn't the only big sports organisation with a president. The difference is that casual sports fans would be hard pressed to name the presidents of the IRFU and the FAI, whereas the president of the GAA is someone who usually has a high profile.

Before Liam O'Neill took the mantle in 2012, it was Christy Cooney's turn. The Corkman was a high-powered executive in FÁS, on a reported salary of nearly €160,000 per annum. This would have meant the GAA paying a near half-million total to FÁS to cover the president's term of office. That led to a few hefty shoulders from various commentators over the course of Cooney's tenure, but the former president doesn't feel that a high wage undercut his credibility on issues such as under-the-counter manager payments.

"It was never something that overly concerned me, because what was I supposed to do? Not get paid? Money has never been an issue for me within the Association. It just so happened I had a very senior job, and that's how it worked out. But I think I brought skill sets to the GAA from that job which were invaluable to the GAA while I was there. It was never an issue about money for me.

"Some people had a perception about it; some hadn't. Some said 'the man is taking three years out of his life for the GAA. Why should he lose financially as a result?' The only thing was, like every other full-time president before me, that you wouldn't lose financially because of it. It was never an issue for me. Every now and again my family would say, 'they're having another cut off you over your pay', and others might say 'would you be better off not taking on the challenge of the role'. But I never saw it that way. I try not to personalise these things. It wasn't an issue for Nickey Brennan and Seán Kelly.

Cooney ties the focus on his wages to the changes in the country: "The financial scene in Ireland changed, circumstances were different—and also, the presidency has a higher profile now. And various things happened to give me a higher profile—the Queen's visit, the funerals in the North, the GPA deal.

"That's life. It's not something that bothers me. If I were doing something wrong, that would have bothered me then. When I went for the presidency everybody knew the job I had with FÁS. Nobody raised it then ... it's not an issue for me. It never was."

PART SIX: EXTERNAL AUDIT

Chapter 30 ∽

THE MOST SIGNIFICANT PURCHASE IN GAA HISTORY

There's an argument that this could have been the very first chapter in the book. Nothing like a bit of context, after all. It sometimes seems that during the debates about professionalism for players which raged a few years ago, and the arguments about paid managers which continue to seethe, there was a whole heap of nonsense being spouted.

Referring to the ethos of the GAA, contributors to those debates occasionally hark back to a pastoral vision of the organisation in the (unspecified) past when players were insulted by proffered expense cheques, tearing them up in outrage, while the notion of pay for play was so outlandish as to provoke laughter. The glory of the little village and the honour of the jersey were all that counted; there were men that time. I tell you now, if they knew what some of these youngsters were looking for etc., etc.

All of this would be endearing if it weren't utter rubbish. Professionalism of one kind—the commercial drive needed to sustain the vast infrastructure of sport—has been ever-present in the GAA. That's hardly surprising. You can't run a 32-county organisation with a presence in practically every parish in the country on goodwill and best wishes. The Association's success in maintaining that presence owes a good deal to hard-headed notions of its worth at all levels of Irish life.

But other versions of professionalism—players being reimbursed for playing, for instance—don't turn out to be too outlandish after all.

———

Historian Paul Rouse of UCD has co-authored, with Mike Cronin and Mark Duncan, some outstanding books about the GAA, including *The GAA: A People's History* and *The GAA: County By County*.

These aren't sports history books; they move beyond the roll-call of honours and achievements which often constitute sports history. They delve into the realities of GAA life, realities which are often either hidden or conveniently forgotten. Rouse is well qualified to comment on the economic history of the GAA.

"You can't look at the history of the GAA without looking at the extraordinary development of modern sport in the nineteenth century, between 1850 and 1900 in particular," he says.

"The establishment of the RFU and the FA in Britain, and those sports which were already established, like cricket and horse racing, expanded extraordinarily in the 1870s and 1880s, and that spread to Ireland as well, where there was a huge growth in the number of cricket, rugby and soccer clubs. And while the establishment of the GAA was in part a reaction against that process, it was also shaped by that process to some extent as well. All around that process was a huge commercial operation. That operation was so extensive, in fact, that you had the professionalisation of soccer in England in the 1880s, just as the GAA was being established. You also had the enclosure of pitches and the charging of people to go in and see athletic events around the same time."

Rouse points out that those developments were part of a continuum of sports commerce. Contrary to the dewy-eyed eulogists of a hard-to-locate Corinthian ideal, there has been commercialism in sport for hundreds of years, he says.

"That's not to say that sport wasn't a commercial proposition before then [the 1880s]. It's been a commercial proposition for centuries. But from the 1850s on there was a concerted effort in Britain to organise and commercialise sport. To commodify it, essentially. And that process spread to Ireland as well. You can't separate the GAA from that. It's part of it whether it's amateur or professional in orientation. The GAA sought grounds to hold matches and athletic events and it charged people to go into those events. That's the first aspect of why money matters."

––––

The whole notion of team sports in Victorian Britain, and particularly their growth in popularity during this period, is linked inextricably to a sense of mission among the upper classes to reform their inferiors, with many of the games used to imbue a muscular Christianity in Britain—and its colonies—having their origin in the exclusive public schools like Eton. Sports like rugby and soccer—short, by the way, for 'Association' the way 'rugger' was short for rugby—trickled downwards from the upper classes, and introducing the class note into the discussion is apt, according to Rouse.

"There were existing sporting clubs in Ireland, particularly athletics—and the GAA was founded primarily to take control of Irish athletics, don't forget. Hurling was there and was important as the symbolic game, but athletics was the widespread game—and the GAA created Gaelic football. You have to look at what was happening in Irish sport around the 1870s in the run-up to the founding of the GAA, when you had two major influences.

"One was the idea of amateurism, and its relationship to professionalism. In the context of the time amateurism was rooted in class—that you had to be a gentleman amateur of a certain class to be involved in a certain type of athletics. The second aspect of the game which was significant was that most of the events organised for these people were organised for Saturdays.

"Look at the early establishment of the GAA and the rhetoric is all about making games available to ordinary people in Ireland. All of

Michael Cusack's and Maurice Davin's writing centred on that, on making sport democratic."

Rouse broadens out that point: "It's an undeniable fact that class mattered all the time in Irish sport. The idea that Ireland is classless is nonsensical; when Irish sport was established in the period from the 1870s to the 1890s Ireland was riven by class, which was intertwined with religion and politics. The greatest marketing success in modern Irish sport is the Munster rugby brand, which is a huge credit to them but is founded on the basic lie that rugby in Munster was always the game of the people. There may be some truth in that, but it's a very partial truth."

Returning to the GAA's engagement with notions of amateurism and professionalism, Rouse shows there's a long lineage to that debate, rooted in the 'collective training' popular among county teams decades ago.

"We had it a hundred years ago. Before the Clare team won their All-Ireland in 1914 they went to train in Lisdoonvarna for a week. Laois would have had a training camp in which they paid the expenses of those who took time off work or who had to get men to go to work for them. The GAA has always been willing to bend with ideas of amateurism. The problem with amateurism has always been to arrive at a definition which is enforceable, and the GAA's approach to all of this has been to take a reasonably fluid attitude to it. The basic tenet is that players should be paid neither a match fee nor a regular wage by the GAA, but around that the margins are fairly hazy."

Rouse's point is a strong one: when county board delegates splutter awake to ignite with anger at annual conventions which bear tales of training weekends at various locations at home and abroad, they'd do well to remember that before they were even born training weekends were a commonplace among inter-county teams. It was just called collective training.

————

We saw earlier in the book how players benefit financially from their high profile within the community, but before doing so we return to the early era mentioned by Rouse, and one of the most significant economic decisions ever taken by the GAA: the purchase of Croke Park.

"Gate receipts within the GAA have been an issue from the start. In the 1880s the GAA owned no field and basically went around trying to rent a field. Every organisation needs money to survive. At that time it wasn't going to get a State grant, obviously, and sponsorship wasn't an option either. The GAA began to acquire fields and charged people admission, but to get people in they did some interesting things. They postered everywhere, for one thing. They put up posters everywhere in the locality before a game advertising who was playing, the price and so on, and they did the same with the local and national press. It was only in the early 1900s that the GAA began to acquire grounds such as the Sportsfield in Thurles and other grounds, but the key to all of this, the massive step forward, was the purchase of Croke Park."

It was badly needed. As Rouse points out, the centrepiece games at inter-county level were a moveable feast: literally moveable in one case at Ashtown Racetrack.

"The importance of the stadium is the fact that almost every All-Ireland final has been played there since the GAA bought it," says Rouse. "The exceptions would be the 1937 hurling final, played in Killarney because Croke Park was being redeveloped; the 1947 football final which was played in New York; and the 1984 hurling final, played in Semple Stadium to commemorate the GAA's centenary. Before that All-Ireland finals were played everywhere: one was played in the Phoenix Park because the grass at Ashtown Racetrack was too long, so they had to pick up the posts and go over to the Phoenix Park. The significance of the move was that venue wasn't enclosed, so an admission fee couldn't be charged, of course.

"All-Ireland finals were played near where the present Donnybrook bus garage stands, and on Maurice Davin's farm in Tipperary where, ironically, Kilkenny won their first All-Ireland. Some All-Irelands were forfeited because teams couldn't agree a venue, but once Croke Park was purchased, that all changed. The GAA used it as a headquarters and revolutionised the ground decade on decade:

putting embankments in place, laying a cinder track, developing the stands and moving from a 10,000 capacity ground with most people standing to an 82,000 capacity with most people sitting. All of that increased its earning capacity, and it also came to be used for national events—the Tailteann Games, the Eucharistic Congress, the 1966 commemoration, the Special Olympics, the Queen's visit . . . the GAA headquarters becomes a national monument, if you like."

———

We won't reach for the obvious cliché about history repeating itself first as tragedy, then as farce. The current economic downturn is a huge challenge for people in all sorts of ways and the GAA is no exception, but Rouse sees parallels between the current economic situation and the eighties. As a consolation, he points out that the fifties, in fact, were worse when it came to emigration.

"There's the age structure of who actually plays the games. You have clubs which are very close to the bone when it comes to fielding players. For some clubs you couldn't overestimate the impact of a family with a few sons or daughters moving into an area. By the same token, if that family emigrates you not only lose the father, who may be involved in the club, you lose the kids. Then there's the importance of summer work for students. We seem to be back in a position where there's no summer work for students, like the eighties, so students go away for the summers to work.

"You'd have to be concerned about the long-term viability of some clubs. Without doubt you're going to have fewer teams, with clubs putting out two teams where they had three, or one where they had two. And you could have lads fulfilling fixtures just to keep clubs going. The one good thing is that the GAA has survived cataclysms before. Take the fifties. At the end of that decade there were 2.9 million people in the country, so it's not as bad as it was then in the numbers sense. We have also had a baby boom, so those are kids who would, you'd imagine, feed through to join the clubs eventually."

There are other challenges. Rouse makes some relevant points about the paid-managers debate, for instance.

"The GPA's been a very successful organisation, inserting itself into the heart of Croke Park and receiving remarkable amounts of revenue from the GAA at a time of declining revenue within the GAA as a whole. It's interesting to me to hear people say that managers should be paid. Who's going to pay them? The ordinary punter who pays into matches? The money has to come from somewhere. If it's in the Association it can be spent on clubs, county teams, managers—there's only a certain amount in the pot. You can say that the pot is generated by TV money and sponsorship, but it's money used to run the organisation as it currently stands, and that's not to get into the situation where some counties can't manage their own finances."

For all that, the historian points out that while there are economic questions the GAA has to answer, there are also compelling notions of identity it has to address—and a sense that addressing the latter may also help in answering the former.

"The story of the GAA—as with all sports organisations—is that it's a constant battle not so much to generate money to maintain the organisation, but to develop itself. Look across the board and the great advantages the GAA has over soccer and rugby are first, the sports, which are magnificent. That's not to say rugby and soccer aren't magnificent, but hurling and football are truly superb.

"The other advantage is the facilities the GAA has around the country. The quality of grounds around the country is an extraordinary resource that other sports don't have. What soccer and rugby have, which the GAA doesn't, is an international TV market which allows them to generate money, so it's swings and roundabouts. To me the big challenge for the GAA is to recreate its presence in the schools and to develop that. And that costs money."

Back where we started a century and a quarter after it all began. But it surely tells you something that the challenges remain the same, even if the GAA's approach to those challenges has changed hugely.

Chapter 31 ⌒

DOES LOTTERY FUNDING LEAD TO ALL-IRELAND SUCCESS?

O riginally this chapter was to trace the long-lost connections between All-Ireland success and National Lottery funding. In true guerrilla-economist style I felt I'd stumbled across the magic bullet that would prove, once and for all, what made the difference in a county's fortunes—those crisp Lottery cheques.

Early in the conversation with John Considine on the matter, however, it became clear that "success" in this area related directly to a county's presence at the Cabinet table and not to the silverware in the trophy cabinet.

"Look, there's no correlation between on-field success and Lottery funding," is Considine's blunt appraisal. "Where Lottery funding does count, though, is in sports capital grants, which is where the GAA does very well because there's a matching funds requirement. The GAA is one of the best organisations around when it comes to raising money which can be matched by the grant, so in that sense the GAA is more likely to benefit from Lottery grants than an inner-city boxing club, for instance.

"The capital grants suit the GAA because they're better organised to take advantage of them. The other reason those types of grants suit the GAA is because generally speaking the clubs have got a field and usually—not always, but usually—the grants are for bricks and mortar projects: clubhouses, dressing-rooms, floodlights. There aren't any wages to be paid, no residual profits to be paid off."

The funding is designed to increase participation, which is a stick that's sometimes used to beat the GAA with. In another chapter of this book Pete Lunn of the ESRI makes a cogent argument about participation levels within the GAA flat-lining, particularly in comparison with other team sports.

Considine flips that accusation around, however, and points it back at the top sports governing body in the country.

"Yes, some people argue that that kind of funding is not directed specifically at participation, which is a big goal of the Lottery funding programme, though to me that's a bit of a one-sided argument. The retort to that could be that the Irish Sports Council itself has received plenty of funding to boost participation in sport, but has participation improved? The Council has conducted research which concludes largely that participation isn't affected by where sports capital grants go, so the GAA could argue 'Why should we have to prove we've increased participation when money spent on that elsewhere hasn't succeeded?'"

Still, nobody would seriously argue that participation is the reason that people sometimes have a problem with sports capital grants and Lottery funding. There's a far more problematic issue involved when it comes to the allocation of that money, and that's the perception of unfairness in distribution.

———

Dr Jim McDaid was sports minister from 1997 to 2002 and John O'Donoghue held that portfolio from 2002 to 2007. As long ago as 2004, Dave Hannigan of *The Sunday Times* scrutinised their disbursement of funds.

O'Donoghue's constituency—rural south Kerry—got more money in one round of funding than counties Cavan, Carlow, Clare, Donegal, Kilkenny, Laois, Leitrim, Longford, Louth, Mayo,

Monaghan, Offaly, Roscommon, Sligo, Waterford, Westmeath and Wicklow; three organisations in O'Donoghue's own backyard, including Laune Rangers GAA club, were given €650,000 between them, a sum in excess of that allocated to three entire counties.

Hannigan described an accompanying "perception at grass-roots level of a pattern of cronyism running through the sports capital grant programme since the day in 1999 when counties Kildare (home of the Minister for Finance, Charlie McCreevy) and Donegal (home of O'Donoghue's predecessor Jim McDaid) received nearly 20 per cent of all funding."

The journalist added that at that point in the history of the funding scheme "St Eunan's of Letterkenny received more money than any one of the other 2,000-plus GAA clubs nationwide." St Eunan's was the club where McDaid once served as chairman. As for the Minister for Finance at the time, Charlie McCreevy was invited to open the swanky new pavilion at Rathcoffey GAA club in 2003. "Affording their local TD that singular honour was the least the north Kildare outfit could do," wrote Hannigan. "After all, between 1999 and 2003, they had received nearly €1m in sports capital grants. In a scheme where half the organisations who apply annually are rejected, they somehow managed to hit the jackpot four years out of five. McCreevy isn't even a member of Rathcoffey. His heart belongs to Kill, the membership of which he lists on his official Dáil profile. Last Friday week, Kill drew down €200,000, completing a remarkable run of success for the minister's club. After making the cut five years out of six, their grant tally since 1999 is now within shouting distance of the €1m mark too."

A Department of Finance press release of the time stated that such allocations demonstrated "the government's on-going support to the development and promotion of sport throughout the country, not least in Co Kildare". As Hannigan pointed out, by that time Kildare had received over €19m from the Department of Arts, Tourism and Sport since 1999.

"It may well be the county with the fastest-growing population in Ireland, but that alone hardly explains why it deserved €8m more than Limerick in the same period," remarked Hannigan. Or €4m more than Galway. Both those counties have larger populations. Neither has a finance minister among their TDs."

———

Clearly this is a pattern of behaviour which no one wants; a situation where your success as a sports club—in any sport—depends on geographical luck.

In addition, Considine's point about the lack of a connection between Lottery funding and success rings true if you look at how the favoured counties have fared.

Jim McDaid's Donegal only won a second All-Ireland senior title in 2012, years after he'd left office. Kildare's 1998 losing final to Galway remains their sole trip to Croke Park in the last half-century. Kerry have had plenty of success in the last decade, but the preceding two counties' lack of visits from Sam Maguire suggests John O'Donoghue's munificence had nothing to do with that.

Considine goes on to point out that when it comes to attitudes towards the dispersal of Lottery funding, you're drifting away from economics and into politics: "Not alone are they not ashamed of it, they're proud of it. John O'Donoghue was elected to represent the people of south Kerry, so why wouldn't he 'look after' the people of south Kerry? You don't want a purely bureaucratic system, and eventually John O'Donoghue is accountable, though you'd have to consider it this way—allocating a lot of funds to Kerry might get him votes there, but he's unlikely to lose a lot of votes elsewhere because of that, because the people elsewhere don't see it going on. The whole system is structured to suit this. As an economist, we teach about people being self-interested, so you couldn't be surprised about it."

There are alternatives, says the UCC academic. There are even common-sense adjustments that could be made to the Lottery distribution model that might be fairer.

"In the UK there's an independent board which allocates funds," says Considine, "but I was on a radio programme once with Jim McDaid, and he made the point, 'don't tell me those boards aren't political'. To me the answer is to put a cap on the present system:

'you can't allocate any county more than one and a half the national average'. Stop it being totally abused. There's a good ranking system in place for projects, but the ultimate decision lies with the Minister. And it's not like there's anything wrong with that, but maybe there should be a constraint on them as well."

How much of it is just a matter of 'to the winner the spoils', though? You win the election; you get to choose?

"That seems to be the way, but is that the way we want to organise society? That's what got us into the mess we're in. If we don't stop then you're on the path to Zimbabwe, where Mugabe happens to win the lottery every week. Is that what we want? But to answer your question, there might be no correlation between success on the field of play and lottery funding, but there is a correlation between success in building new facilities and lottery funding all right."

And between county allocations and ministerial presence. Even as this book was being finished, the Minister of State with responsibility for sport, Michael Ring of Mayo, was in the limelight when news broke of Mayo getting a surge of 70 per cent in its allocation of Lottery-funded capital sports grants in 2011.

The funding doesn't just cover sports projects—youth activities, education, environment, health and Irish language projects are also included—but €678,000 of the €1.8 million the county received was channelled through Ring's department: his home town of Westport received three grants totalling €230,000, more than the whole of south county Dublin.

"Think about it," says Considine. "Mayo didn't do that well for a long time with those grants. So . . ." Say no more.

Chapter 32 ∿

AN AGNOSTIC'S VIEW OF GAA FUNDING

You may or may not recall a storm in a teacup some years ago following the publication of an ESRI report on participation in sport.

The Sporting Lives report caused quite a bit of comment because of its adverse findings about GAA participation levels. The ESRI defended itself when the GAA questioned the report, and there were high noon meetings in the Irish Sports Council (ISC) offices, as one participant describes it.

Does that sound a little over the top? Take a second and come at it from the economic angle, thinking only of this term: sports capital grants. The GAA has always been hugely successful in attracting same, and this report threatened the possibility of that success stretching into the future.

———

Pete Lunn of the ESRI revisits the controversy calmly, now that the gun-smoke is a distant memory. Lunn's voice is distinctive, by which I mean he has a noticeable English accent; you might ask why each contributor's speaking voice isn't detailed to the same extent, but we'll get to that, or rather, Lunn himself will.

"We produced a statistical reconstruction of grass-roots sport over a period of 30 or 40 years for the Irish Sports Council," he says. "We didn't know what the result would be and we were surprised by the results we got—quite shocked, really. We had a really good sample of people recall their sporting history, over 3,000 people—if they'd played sport at any time in their lives regularly, what it was, what age they took it up, when they dropped out, and so on.

"We reconstructed their sporting histories from that sample and the results showed that there had been a huge growth in the amount of sporting activity, with modern adults playing much more sport as children and adults, with sport being pretty loosely defined as per the ISC's definition. The reason behind the looseness of the definition is that the primary goal of sports policy is to improve people's health, though there may be a secondary goal involving the social aspect of sport.

"One finding was that while there'd been a huge growth in sports participation, it was in individual rather than team sports which had really taken off—jogging, cycling, golf, swimming—that kind of thing. The traditional team sports didn't have the same levels of growth, but the area where growth had primarily taken place was in soccer, and among kids in particular."

At first glance this doesn't look like great news for the GAA, but neither does it look like a reason to cut down goalposts all over Ireland either. Lunn prefers to run through the methodology used by the ESRI by way of expansion and, more importantly perhaps, the phraseology the organisation used: "What we found was that the GAA was flat-lining, effectively, with Gaelic games not increasing in popularity. They weren't losing popularity; they had the same proportion of people playing them—that's a generalisation but it's pretty accurate—while almost all other sports were growing.

"We described that conclusion and thought about that from a policy point of view. What we chose to do was we decided to say that Gaelic games were in relative decline, quickly adding what we meant: that other sports were growing faster than they were and they were accounting for a smaller market share when it came to Irish sport. And of course it rather blew up in our faces."

Lunn exhales. "It was a very unpopular message."

―――――

From the word go Lunn found himself arguing the case for his report. Curiously enough, for an organisation that often sees itself as battling the media, in this case the GAA found outlets for its annoyance in the very same sector, says the researcher.

"We ended up having to defend the report before it was even published because people in the GAA picked up the phone to friends in the newspapers and said the report was rubbish because they felt their sports were expanding. It was entirely understandable that they would perceive their sports to be expanding because the population, and particularly the population of young people, was expanding over the last ten or 20 years. Consequently they'd be almost bound to see the numbers involved expand, but we were looking at proportions of people playing different sports.

"When I said they were flat-lining that's what I meant. If the total population increases then participation increases, so you're likely to have more clubs and participants. I wish I'd made that point at the time, but I know more now than I did about Irish demography."

Lunn still stands over the numbers he and his colleagues got to crunch, and the policy recommendation implied by those numbers, which was the crux of the matter.

"There was nothing wrong with the data. We relied on people's memories, but we plotted the trends forward and matched it to other modern surveys, and the end points of the trends matched those other modern surveys perfectly. We had no reason to doubt the numbers. They were rock solid.

"As a result we said it was very difficult to justify current spending policy because the lion's share of the funding was going to team sports, and to the GAA in particular. We produced numbers on that and I analysed the grants being given through the sports capital programme later, between 1999–2002, when the GAA was getting one-third of all funding. That was difficult to justify in a context where their sports weren't growing and other sports were: at that stage Gaelic football was ranked as the sixth most popular sport and hurling around ninth, yet they were getting one-third of all sports funding. We pointed out that this didn't look like the most efficient use of public money."

Hence the anger in Croke Park. Those retaliatory attacks were on one level, then, an attempt to protect the organisation's funding.

"Of course," says Lunn. "We're used to this in the ESRI. If you come up with findings that an organisation doesn't agree with, the first thing they do is dispute the findings. There was a round played out in public with lots of coverage. I spent quite a bit of time on radio arguing with people from the GAA and saying 'please don't shoot the messenger'."

Lunn adds that he didn't carry an animus against the Association into his research, pointing out that the GAA could have learned from the ESRI's research instead of simply hitting back.

"I'd love the GAA to attract more participants, and I was appealing to the GAA to look at the research and to try to find out why. We've pointed out that the GAA has a real problem with people dropping out in their teens compared to soccer, which tends to hold people into their twenties, thirties and even their forties. I'd love to do more research on Gaelic games and we're still hopeful they'll pitch in and engage with us so we can do that. We feel we could give some good suggestions on how they might turn those trends around."

The usual point made regarding the sports capital grants, of course, was that it was inherently biased towards bricks and mortar projects. According to this logic a rowing club, for instance, wouldn't be building a new tributary of the Lee or the Shannon to practise on, whereas GAA clubs need grounds on which to play, dressing-rooms for their participants, and so on. Lunn points out, however, that poor facilities aren't a bar to progress for a sporting body.

"That's a valid point and one that we made. We showed pretty conclusively in a previous report that facilities were no longer an issue in Irish sport. It used to be the case that facilities were an issue in Irish sport. There was a deficit of facilities, but by the time we carried out a survey in 2003 and asked people if they had difficulty finding facilities or whether the facilities were good, there wasn't a problem. If you asked people if the reason they didn't participate was down to facilities, practically nobody said it was. That result's been repeated several times since.

"You're right—if you're going to focus sports policy on building stuff, there's bound to be a bias towards sports which have to have that kind of infrastructure. What we were suggesting was that given the trends in participation that we saw, the funding had to move away from infrastructure and towards sports development officers—more to people, or as we said at the time, towards social and human capital and away from physical capital. The key to participation was organisation—organising participation around people's busy lives.

"When we looked at what was stopping people from participating in sport, it tended to be time—'I've got a family; I've got a job', so we suggested that instead of providing more dressing-rooms and floodlights for sports that aren't really growing, we should take sports that are growing and find ways to give people more opportunities to participate which took on board the fact that they had busy lives."

The obvious question, then, is how did the report actually affect the GAA's funding?

"The [Irish Sports] Council was certainly receptive to the research and they were aware it would cause some difficulties for some of their other stakeholders, that they would take some heat, but they stuck with it. It was hard not to, because the numbers were plain as day and it was very hard to argue with those.

"We were starting on the assumption that what we care about here is getting people active and participating. If, instead, we care about preserving traditional organisations and we care more about social capital in terms of having people stand on the touchline and drink in the bar than in getting people physically active, then those are perfectly reasonable policy positions to take. We took no stance on that—we took the stated aims of sports policy, which is that the taxpayer pays for this because it's good for us. We made that point—that you could make other arguments, but you needed to be clear about your evidence base. The ISC took that on board. Policy hasn't changed that much, though I think our research did have an impact in terms of broadening their view of funding and how to use it, and in supporting local sports partnerships."

And of course there's also the little matter of context. Although the report is only a few years old, the small matter of the downturn moved the goalposts, to use an apposite cliché. "It's worth making the point that all of this applies to the pre-recession policy," says Lunn. "What happens now that much of that money is cut, and that the ISC must choose how to spend a dwindling budget is another issue."

———

A lot went on after the report was published that people didn't pick up on, however. Just bubbling under the surface there was a stat-off, of sorts. The GAA commissioned a Trinity statistician to write a paper pointing out why the ESRI paper didn't stand up. The Institute responded to that and then there was what Lunn calls "a High Noon type meeting in the ISC at which we rebutted the points made by the statistician". This was six months after the report was published.

"The GAA said it would go away and look at the figures and we haven't heard from them since," says Lunn. "They fought their corner and fought it very hard. Eventually in that meeting they accepted that our numbers were right; we answered the statistician's points and then the GAA said we had used the wrong language to describe them. We said we'd thought long and hard about the language we wanted to use and that we'd used the term 'relative decline' and immediately defined that as saying the GAA was not growing as fast as other sports and was therefore losing market share, or was accounting for a smaller proportion of Irish sport.

"They said our language was inappropriate. We asked what language we should have used, but they went away and we never heard from them again." And if the GAA picked up the phone now, even, and rang Lunn's number in the ESRI, what kind of reaction would they get from the statistician after those bruising few months?

"I'd be delighted," he says. "That's how soccer responded, incidentally. The report was not as bad as it was for the GAA when you came to soccer, but it wasn't great either. Soccer wasn't growing as fast as other sports and it was getting a lot of funding. But they invited me to their HQ to make a presentation, and we crunched a few numbers for them because they were looking for more details, particularly on the gender bias against women in soccer, which was bigger than other team sports like rugby and GAA.

"Since then we've done a report on swimming for Swim Ireland and we're offering to do the same for various governing bodies, including the GAA. I'd like to analyse the data in terms of people dropping out and work out the causes of that—and what the GAA and the ISC could do to help people play these games longer."

Retention of players is the issue, as Lunn sees it: "That's the problem for the GAA. They get a lot of kids playing—not as many as they used to, but that's kind of inevitable with all the other opportunities kids have—and the key is to hold the people they get. I'd love to do more research in that area. It's a matter of constructive engagement."

Lunn remarks that that English background may not have aided his cause with the GAA, but he wasn't that much of a stranger to the Association. When his folks came over to visit from across the water, he took them to a game in Croke Park, but his connection to the GAA went back further.

"I'm sure my accent didn't help," he says. "The irony is I really like Gaelic games. I've been one of those parents who brought their kids down to hurling and football games at the local club, standing on the touchline, and they were a great bunch of people."

Is it too late for the GAA to make cause with someone who was clearly regarded as public enemy number one just a couple of years ago? Not according to the man himself. You'd think that someone in Jones's Road would be well advised to give the ESRI a bell even now.

PART SEVEN: THE LOCAL FRANCHISE

Chapter 33 ∿

SOME JUST AREN'T GOING TO SURVIVE: THE CLUB IN THE FUTURE

Part of the challenge for the GAA facing into the future is the sense of a disconnect between Croke Park and the ordinary club member. It's a subject that I've touched on elsewhere in the book, but for a definitive view the men to talk to were those who'd gone from the rank and file to the top of the pyramid. For his part, Nickey Brennan wasn't wearing the notion of a gulf between the decisions taken at GAA headquarters and those at club level at all.

"I and a number of others did a deal with Google while I was president, and every club in the country was set up with an account. Right now every club secretary, chairman and PRO has a GAA email account, and they get communications from Croke Park on a regular basis. Any club which says it's not being made aware of what's going on in Croke Park . . .

"I went through the statistics relating to club secretaries picking up their emails and so on—as it happens, by far the best county for that was Cork. Many people see Cork as a conservative county in GAA terms, but I'd attribute that success to the current vice-chairman, Ger Lane. All their communications with their clubs are by email now."

Then why is the lament frequently heard that club members are kept in the dark about the GAA and its plans? Brennan has an idea about that: "The point is that there's no shortage of information available to clubs. I don't buy that. What may be happening, maybe, is this—does the secretary keep that information to himself, or does he understand it? What's becoming more and more important in the GAA—it's something that was probably always important—is the kind of person who is taking on officer roles within the Association. Are they able to digest the information they're getting and disseminate it?

"I don't buy the line that Croke Park doesn't communicate with the clubs; I'd ask if the secretary disseminates that, or does he even open those emails in the first place? Does he understand the ramifications of that decision for his club? That might be a more relevant question. In my time we also introduced the newsletter to inform clubs on what was happening, so that's another channel of information."

————

Enda McGuane makes the point that the chairmen of some GAA clubs have a habit of leaving messes after them when they step down, an unfortunate version of legacy debt that newly elected officials then face.

Brennan argues the case for a "rolling strategic plan" to act as an automatic brake on extravagance and indicts any club which doesn't have one.

"If it doesn't (have a plan) then it lacks direction. Such a plan would look at the capabilities of the club to invest or for teams to progress, and the chairman should be allowed to put his stamp on it, but it must be there and it has to roll on to the next man. In fairness I think clubs are getting better on that, but the important thing to bear in mind is that any club—or county board—going to borrow money from a bank has to have the imprimatur of the GAA. And the GAA will not give that unless it sees that strategic plan, so the whole thing is a lot tighter now than it was, and clubs can't just go out and borrow as they want."

The Kilkenny native goes along with Paudie Butler's suggestion that clubs need to move away from cajoling people into accepting officerships they don't really want to take up and should start persuading members to take up short-term projects instead. He also acknowledges an occasional reluctance among some club officers to embrace openness, to put it politely.

"The key is the capability of the people leading clubs. I'm not referring to anyone specific here, but there are people running clubs who can't run their own house at home, while there are other people in clubs who are senior people in management—who understand time management, delegation, measuring projects.

"Of course the GAA is a mixture of all of those, and it'd be unfair to expect every club to have a wizard for every position. But senior officers must have the ability to work within the team at club officer level. There's nothing inhibiting clubs from doing what Paudie is saying—'we want a hurling wall built. Johnny, Jim and Jack, you three tease it out and come back to us with a proposal.' But there are people with the attitude, 'I must keep all of this inside' and if you have that kind of person you'll have a problem running the club. But if you have someone with trust in others you'll have more people involved in projects like that and the club will be more vibrant. You'd have to admit, though, that as an Association we've had people at times who wanted everything under their own control. That's not tenable nowadays."

The ultimate loss of control would be the disappearance of the club. But what about amalgamations? Brennan's on the record as saying that some clubs will have to amalgamate or die—partly due to another major social change.

"Clubs kept going through the bad days of the thirties and the fifties and even the eighties, but even in the eighties you had relatively large families. The problem now is that apart from emigration, you're dealing with a smaller cohort of children coming through. Whether we like it or not, there's competition from other leisure pursuits compared to the thirties, forties and fifties, in particular, when the GAA almost had a monopoly on numbers.

"That's no longer the case. Now, people make style choices. You and I might love the competitive nature of Gaelic games because we were reared on that, but people nowadays don't necessarily appreciate that. They want their kids to play sport, but they may not want them in competitive sport; that's a big difference." (Brennan's right, if a Munster Council report is to be believed—that parents value a safe environment and their kids' sociability over sporting excellence.)

The net result is that some "are just not going to survive", says Brennan.

"Now, if my club had to amalgamate with another club, then I'd probably be crying for a week, but a person who doesn't see the obvious isn't doing much for his club. The reality is that some clubs are going to have to amalgamate because the numbers simply are not there. County boards can run competitions down to 11 a side in an effort to keep games going, but to me that's just putting off the evil day.

"Unfortunately the bigger issue isn't the amalgamation of the two teams. It's the fact that both of them probably have a pitch and dressing-rooms or other property which can lead to 'we'll train here this week and the other place the next week', and you end up keeping two premises on the go."

He pauses. "You're back to economics again."

———

Seán Kelly immediately echoes Brennan's point on club premises.

"At the moment it's probably too late, but some of the ventures that clubs embarked on were too ambitious. In some cases clubs had nice grounds in the middle of their town or village, central to the community, but they sold those off to move outside their immediate catchment area. Some of those clubs are in bother at the moment because the bigger the new facilities are, the harder they are to keep going costwise. An overall strategy is needed for every region, because obviously what'll work in Dublin won't necessarily work in west Cork or Kerry. You must cut your cloth."

He feels those mistakes are "few and far between", but that doesn't mean the resolution will be ideal.

"Eventually the mistakes will probably have to be absorbed by the GAA, which isn't the best thing in the world. When I was president I was able to say to the banks that the GAA never had a bad debt; no GAA club or county board ever walked away without paying. That was very important looking for loans, to maintain that good name. If you couldn't maintain it, then obviously circumstances changed."

That's another twist to the relationship between the club and Croke Park, of course; sometimes the club's actions can impact on GAA HQ rather than the other way round. And when the context is financial, that can be . . . awkward.

———

Asked how the atmosphere is when the banks sit down to talk to senior GAA officials, Kelly says most of the time it's good.

"That's because a lot of the time the bank would be clever enough to put people there for you to deal with who are involved themselves in the GAA, people who understand the GAA. I had one or two tough meetings with higher-ups in the banks, particularly a meeting in relation to an issue relating to Fitzgerald Stadium. We got annoyed. The man we were dealing with certainly wasn't a GAA man and tried to come the heavy on us a small bit. We stood up to him and got better terms.

"The GAA gets fair play, by and large. The number of problems we'd have with the banks would be few and far between—obviously at the highest level they'd be keen to hang on to the accounts because they're so big. And we'd have fairly good experts within the Association to deal with banking issues, people who'd be well able to match the banks word for word."

Neatly enough, Kelly articulates one concern which is often heard in club bars and function rooms: the supposed army of workers the GAA employs in Croke Park.

"Something else the GAA has to be careful of is not to take on too many employees. There have been huge developments in, say, employing coaches in recent years. The more full-time employees you take on, though, the less flexibility you have as an organisation, because you'll have a bottom line to meet then every year.

"I have no problem with coaches, but an amateur organisation has to be conscious of that fact. If you take on coaches they fill a void, but if they go then will that void be filled? You have to be careful to balance the two, the amateur and the full-time, because it's easy to go for the full-time man in times of plenty, but what happens when the money dries up?"

Ultimately Kelly sees the danger of that disconnect, but feels it's more perception than reality.

"The one thing you look at is whether each individual full-time employee is involved with his or her own club on a voluntary basis. Those that are should be fairly in touch with what's happening. Those who aren't, then that mightn't be helpful. But I think most of them would be. Personally I wouldn't be in favour of taking on anyone full-time unless they were prepared to do something, or to have done something, on a voluntary basis. You might have some people with very specific technical expertise that wouldn't be involved, but it's hard to see how any full-time employee of an organisation run on a voluntary basis shouldn't be prepared himself to do something on a voluntary basis. If that's your benchmark you won't lose touch.

"There's bound to be some distance between Croke Park and the grass roots, but that's true of every large centralised organisation—the civil service, the FAI—you could say it of every organisation. But at the same time you must keep the connection as close as possible, because a disconnect will turn people off and they'll walk away."

Chapter 34 ∾

SPLITS NEEDED: WHY SUPERCLUBS ARE BAD NEWS FOR DUBLIN

We've seen Dublin's significance loom large in other sections of this book—Páraic Duffy's comments on their importance in terms of boosting the GAA's hand in signing broadcasting deals is just one example. The vast crowds of spectators filling Croke Park are good news—good economic news—that isn't restricted to the publicans in Drumcondra and its environs.

But having a catchment area with over one million people isn't always a blessing. Counties which see busloads of people emigrate—many of them to Dublin and no further, come to that—mightn't agree, but huge numbers bring their own challenges. It's always hard to teach in a crowded classroom, and there's always a chance that a talented kid isn't given a chance to shine.

———

In the wider scheme of things there is no denying the importance of the men in sky blue to the GAA's financial health. They used to say in America that what was good for General Motors was good for the country, and there can be a sense that what's good for the Dubs—namely, winning games—is good for the GAA.

John Considine says unprompted that the GAA would obviously want Dublin to keep on winning, but he points out that the GAA outposts in other urban centres in the country would also benefit hugely from similar success.

"In the last ten years there has been no game, before an All-Ireland semi-final or final, with an attendance of over 50,000 that Dublin has not been involved in," says Considine. "So in that sense the GAA would want Dublin to keep winning. But if Dublin keep winning their supporters would get bored and stop coming. What would be more important for the GAA as a whole would be seeing the Wexford and Limerick hurlers getting on a roll, because traditionally those counties draw very big support when they start winning games. You're also talking about cities, big population centres—if you got Limerick and Wexford going you'd make a difference

"Galway have rugby, a few teams in the second tier of the League of Ireland, and there's a geographical divide in terms of hurling and football. There isn't a tradition of going to hurling games. Why? Because they wouldn't have had a Connacht championship to go to.

"The best time for hurling attendances was the late nineties, when unsuccessful counties broke through and the Big Three were hungry for success. Clare and Tipperary were filling the Pairc, Offaly were winning All-Irelands, Limerick were in an All-Ireland . . . it was never better."

But back to Dublin. The population is there, and lately there are two competitive teams at the top level in hurling and Gaelic football. As Considine points out, though, if those sides were to dominate for the next few years, people would be turned off. Would Dublin losing an All-Ireland semi-final or final by a point, with a new county coming through to the decider every year instead, be the optimum narrative for attendances?

"Yes," says Considine. "It's a strange mix. People want to watch champions. But they also want a challenger. If you could script it you could work that in, but obviously you can't. You need characters and incident, upsets, a rallying cause. I think people like stats and so on but they love the human interest stories.

"People identify with teams. If you sat down and analysed it, why do people identify with Manchester United when they're not from Manchester? For instance, people would identify more naturally in Cork with the hurlers than the footballers, for whatever reason, but when the footballers finally won the All-Ireland there was a huge outpouring of emotion. They'd had heartbreaks and upsets along the way, and a lot of counties were hoping they'd win—not because they were against Down, but because they'd battled so long to make it."

Fair enough, the narrative favoured Dublin in 2011. Can they build on that for the future? One big issue is the club situation in the capital.

———

"It's a funny one," says Mick O'Keeffe. "I won't say it's a dangerous situation, but it's awkward."

O'Keeffe is talking about clubs in Dublin, and the huge suburban outfits in particular. These have superseded the inner-city clubs, and while Dublin were holding the Sam Maguire when we spoke, how good is the dominance of those superclubs for the GAA in Dublin as a whole?

"There are six or seven of them (superclubs)—Lucan, St Brigid's, Kilmacud, Ballyboden—and all of them are in the suburban ring around the city," says O'Keeffe. "The likes of Cuala in Dalkey, St Sylvester's in Malahide, Fingallians in Swords—they have a huge pick. Someone said to me that St Brigid's have a bigger pick than Limerick. The other side of that is that you have clubs on their knees, squeezed into tiny areas—in one part of Dublin you have Scoil Uí Chonaill, Raheny, Clontarf, Trinity Gaels, Naomh Barrog, St Monica's, O'Toole's—all in about a three mile area. Those clubs can't get out their own minor teams, some of them. Then in Kilmacud you have four U21 teams. That means one hundred lads just at that level. At some underage levels they're fielding six teams, and players are getting lost."

This is a familiar situation in other urban centres, with power drifting out from the traditional inner-city strongholds to the commuter dormitories—it's happened in Cork, in Waterford. The one difference with Dublin is that it's not as if GAA coverage spreads evenly over the capital, says O'Keeffe.

"You have black spots, places which just aren't GAA areas. Beann Eadair out in Howth have an adult team and a couple of underage teams because while they have a big population base, it just isn't a GAA area. Some clubs in Dublin are in dire straits, while you have those half a dozen superclubs. I think we might be in danger of losing sight of what success is for some of the junior clubs in Dublin. Success for some of them is putting a junior team on the field, while for Kilmacud Crokes success is winning the All-Ireland club final.

"The traditional powerhouses in Dublin would have been St Vincent's, Clan na Gael in Ringsend, Crumlin in hurling, O'Tooles were originally from the Five Lamps—but now the strong clubs are in Kilmacud, Dalkey, Templeogue, Blanchardstown. All the commuter towns. All the population.

"Vincent's is fascinating. Where they're based was a suburb with fields around it 40 years ago, but now it's in the city. What they benefit from is that Vincent's people in Portmarnock or Malahide will bring their kids in to play for them, though. But generally it's a numbers game, and the city clubs don't have the numbers."

What's the answer? Simple. More clubs. Or more splits in the ones which exist already.

———

Páraic Duffy nods when you raise the issue. Inter-county players are the marquee names, of course, but in a vast urban area GAA clubs—Saturday morning training for small kids, summer camps—are the visible face of the organisation rather than a player who may spend his entire playing career obscured by a hurling helmet.

His first observation is a simple one: "There's a broader issue with Dublin clubs, of course—we just don't have enough of them in Dublin. There are less than one hundred clubs here. Cork has twice as many clubs as Dublin."

Duffy echoes O'Keeffe on the huge clubs dotted around the city, but he points out that while the GAA needs to create new clubs, it's not straightforward. If there are advantages to having the country's largest catchment area to draw from, that comes with drawbacks as well.

"What we have are more and more massive clubs—Ballyboden, Na Fianna, Kilmacud—and that's not a good model. We're finding it desperately difficult to establish new clubs in Dublin, particularly in areas with huge populations, and we've tried. See, we're coming back to the economics of it again, because starting a GAA club is expensive. Lads can start a soccer team quite easily—a set of jerseys and borrowing a pitch.

"A GAA club needs a ground, clubhouse, community activities, insurance . . . it's expensive. There's been a growth in participation in Dublin, but it's based on clubs getting bigger and bigger. We've increased the numbers but not the clubs, and that's a huge problem."

Ironically, the road to success may lie in internal division. Brendan Behan used to say the first item on any Irish organisation's agenda was the split. Duffy wishes that observation was more accurate, based on the evidence north of the Liffey.

"Look at what happened in St Brigid's," he says. "There was a row and Castleknock GAA club was founded, which is now a great area for us because you have two very good clubs. Someone said that that's what we need in Dublin—a series of rows within clubs to split the huge clubs up. Castleknock GAA club is growing well, but it's helped because St Brigid's was growing so fast.

"There's another complication now in Dublin in that you can't say 'we'll buy 40 acres of land here and start a club' because the local authorities are pressed for cash. I thought we were making progress in that regard a few years ago, but things have changed since, obviously."

At the other end of the scale, clubs in remote rural areas are struggling for numbers and may need to amalgamate to survive. It's not an issue in the capital, obviously, but it illustrates the range of challenges facing the GAA nationally.

"That's beginning to happen already," says Duffy. "We've had requests for amalgamation, and unfortunately that's going to happen more and more, which isn't good for us. The problem is making the change. Dublin needs more clubs. Amalgamation needs to happen among clubs on the west coast. But making these things happen is desperately difficult—that's the bind. It's the culture versus the economic reality all over again."

Isn't it always?

Chapter 35

WHY THE SPECTRUM OF CONCERN MEANS A COUNTY BOARD SPENDING CAP IS A GOOD IDEA

W hen this book was being proposed, the notion of a spending cap for county boards was on the light-hearted end of the scale. Imagine a county secretary cutting back on the half-time oranges! Or leaving those floodlights off until it's nearly throw-in time. (Let them warm up in the corridor under the stands!)

Of course, by the time the book was up and running county board expenditure was no longer a light-hearted issue, but one which was exercising a lot of minds, given the evidence to hand.

For instance . . . at the end of 2011 a deficit of €220,000 was revealed at Tipperary's annual convention in Thurles, while spending on inter-county teams exceeded the €1m mark for a fourth successive year.

In their run to the All-Ireland senior hurling final Tipperary spent €1,171,876 on inter-county teams, down €61,516 from the 2010 figure of €1,233,392, which was an all-time high. Yet that €61,516 was offset by a drop of 18 per cent in gate receipts from local games—from €323,000 in 2010 to €263,605 in 2011; income from the county senior hurling championship dropped by over €100,000 in the last three years.

Mayo also had serious problems in 2011, owing over €10 million to the bank, a situation so grave that Ulster Bank officials went directly to Croke Park and asked officials there to put in place a repayment structure.

They weren't alone, of course. Another big county suffered a big blow in 2012—the Kildare County Board needed an advance from Croke Park of €300,000 to meet its obligations, while its loan payment schedule was extended from the original date of 2014 to 2017 (the board were also given the expertise of Simon Moroney of the Munster Council, who was immediately likened to A.J. Chopra of the International Monetary Fund at a Kildare County Board meeting).

Waterford had a rough 2012, with officials within the county battling for much of the year to stem rumblings about the finances within the county: coping with the fall-out from fundraising concerts which lost thousands, and denying reports that players' expense cheques had bounced. (Former GAA president Nickey Brennan has a novel idea to solve some of Waterford's problems, but that comes later in this book.)

Leaving aside loose comparisons to the head of the IMF, practically every week in 2012 there were suggestions that county boards all over the country were in trouble. Surely a spending cap was a good idea, then?

———

Enda McGuane sees the point immediately and isn't long making comparisons that go far beyond these shores. The best example of how a spending cap—or more precisely, a salary cap—works is in American team sports.

"Look at Major League Baseball or the National Football League in America, and they have spending caps, limits to what you can spend on your team in terms of salary. That's it and you have to live within your resources. The aim is to create competition, and the salary caps and so on ensure the leagues are competitive and there are different teams winning, and when a team wins it doesn't get a great draft pick, which means the playing field is pretty level.

"In the GAA it's different because for one thing a lot of the fundraising mechanisms would have to be centralised—supporters' clubs and so on. Then you'd look at what's on the table, and you can make a decision when you see exactly what's involved. It's interesting, though, because a question you'd have to ask is this—how much is enough to spend preparing a team? That's a thorny political issue."

McGuane's right. There are several issues which intersect here for the GAA—manager payments, player preparation and county board expenditure. All too often one of those tends to dominate, and it isn't the long-suffering treasurer who has to sign off on those team-bonding weekends.

"There are managers who'll say they'll spend whatever it takes to win an All-Ireland, but the reality is you must look at the long-term fundamentals too," says McGuane. "If you look at county board expenditures and compare what they're spending on the preparation of county teams and what's being put into coaching and games development for kids, there's a considerable gap between the two which has to be addressed. Obviously the GAA generates considerable revenue and the All-Ireland finals are the peak, but inter-county players represent the very small top of the pyramid. The organisation was set up to promote the games to everyone, so that's an area we have to look at."

McGuane points out that there is now an entire "industry" devoted to the preparation of teams. That industry isn't always tuned to the specific needs of Gaelic football and hurling teams.

"I was on the Clare football team for five years while I was based in Mullingar, for instance. The one thing you hear from professional athletes all the time is that the most important part of preparation is the rest factor; if you don't rest you don't get the benefits of training. Yet a GAA player can't take that rest—he's into work at 9 am the morning after a training session.

"Is that beneficial? Would you achieve more by doing less? That's a discussion that should happen, because nowadays the attitude to training seems to be 'they're doing it so we should be doing it'. But a one-size-fits-all model doesn't work when it comes to sports training.

"Sports science should lead the GAA that way—the man who wins the Olympic gold medal for the triathlon is probably one of the fittest people in the world, but he wouldn't do much for you on a hurling or football team. There's a whole industry out there involved in the preparation of teams. We have to accept that, and it's something that'll become more evident in the next couple of years."

––––

Páraic Duffy sets the individual challenges facing county boards in the context of a "spectrum" of concerns. After all, his appointment as director-general came at an interesting time, to use the Chinese application of that term.

"How much time is taken up, then, by economic challenges? More now than when I started which was 2008, when the economic crisis really took hold—I was unfortunate to some degree," says Duffy with a wry smile. "Obviously that's had a huge impact on us, because I'd be lying if I said we didn't have financial challenges in many of our counties and clubs. We have about 15 clubs that we are working with the banks on while we scrutinise county board expenditure more closely now than ever, and we'd be concerned about quite a few of them. We're managing it reasonably well. Kildare grabbed the headlines recently, but there are other counties in a difficult situation. I think the penny has dropped with counties this year that they have to cut their costs. I think we'll get out of it okay, but we're keeping a close eye on some counties."

Duffy ranks the county boards in three different tiers when it comes to levels of concern. "We go through the various issues with a new president, and when he came in we had a three hour meeting on the financial end of things with Liam O'Neill and we went through the 32 counties with him because we know the financial situation with every one of them.

"I'll be frank, there's a spectrum of concern. In broad terms there are ten you'd be worried about; there'd be ten or 11 in the middle breaking even; and there'd be another ten or 11 that you'd have no worries about."

What makes the difference for these administrators? Is good housekeeping crucial? Or, to be blunt about it, if you're a one-code county that makes a short run in the championship, are you just better off?

"Essentially it's good management. A county like Cork would generate significant income—which they will need for the redevelopment of Pairc Uí Chaoimh—and especially from their local championships. A county like Sligo, for instance, would have low returns from their local championships. Dublin again is different . . . it has sponsorship opportunities and so on that aren't available to other counties.

"But above all it's down to good financial management. Any county can make ends meet if it has good financial management, but what's happened in some counties is that they've spent for success. I'm not blaming managers here, but there have been huge investments and careless management in some counties in relation to county teams."

Huge investments and careless management might sound like a mantra for the entire country over the last ten years or so, but it can be lethal for a county board. Duffy's choice of the term 'careless' is accurate, if kind.

Huge investments, at least, have generally left a concrete legacy. The urge to build during the boom wasn't confined to over-eager property developers, and the plethora of new and redeveloped grounds might explain why an end has come, more or less, to infrastructural development within the GAA, as we shall see.

PART EIGHT: FUTURE OUTLOOK

Chapter 36 ∿

THE DON DRAPER APPROACH: REBRANDING THE GAA

Having landed the windfall of soccer and rugby revenue when Lansdowne Road was being refurbished, it's not surprising that many within the GAA see the return of the two national teams as an obvious way for the Association to reap another financial reward.

Equally, it's not surprising that the man who facilitated rugby and soccer being played in Croke Park sees that happening again. Seán Kelly argues that simple common sense dictates it.

"It's not practical at this point in time because the IRFU and the FAI have commitments to the Aviva. My club, Kilcummin, though, put through a motion two years ago to have Croke Park opened permanently, and it went through on the nod, basically. I expect to see big rugby matches back in Croke Park. Why would you play matches at a 45,000-seater stadium when there's an 82,000-seater available? Over the next few years I expect to see some of the bigger games go back to Croke Park.

"And when the soccer team get a good run, which they will in due course, you could have the bigger teams playing in Croke Park.

But I don't think that'll happen at the moment because of those organisations' commitments to the Aviva."

Kelly offers this view of the importance of that potential cash injection to the GAA. "Money isn't everything, but money's important. The fact that the motion to open Croke Park went through without debate, and almost without publicity—particularly when you compare the publicity surrounding the original opening of Croke Park—is indicative of two things: that people saw the benefits of the good will, but also that counties benefited financially. As the money started drying up, I think those counties realised 'we could do with that money again to promote our own games by employing coaches and so forth'. Money is certainly a factor."

If rugby and soccer return to Jones's Road, the revenue won't be put into building new stadiums around the country. Kelly agrees with the general view on the GAA's stock of big venues.

"We have too many big stadiums. You can't shut them down, so you have to keep them going. There have been redevelopment works in many, which should keep things going for 20 to 30 years, and things will hopefully be better when they need to be redeveloped again. That's particularly important with the prospect of the World Cup coming up in rugby. That'll be an opportunity for revenue which didn't exist before."

————

The return of the boys in green doesn't mean a nice cheque landing in the account of every club in the country, mind. That was mooted back in 2006 when the original decision to open Croke Park was taken, and Nickey Brennan was one of those firmly against that idea.

"With the opening of Croke Park there was debate about what to do with the rugby and soccer money, with suggestions that the bottom line would be divided by the number of clubs in the country, all of which would receive a cheque in due course. I was absolutely opposed to that and put a proposal to Central Council that a specific amount would be given to each county board for specific projects, with the rest ring-fenced for other specific projects to be decided later. I always felt that the legacy of rugby and soccer in Croke Park should be grounds or investment of that type. And that's what happened— we gave €100,000 to each county board and the rest was retained for a special fund for projects.

"Now there were people in clubs unhappy with that. They wanted the (cheques-to-the-clubs) idea, but that would just have saved on fundraising for one year, maybe, and there would have been no legacy at the end of the day. But we were lucky then. Times were good economically and we were storing money, if you want to put it that way."

Brennan acknowledges the difference between those times and the atmosphere in the country as this book was being written.

"With the exception of the last two or three months of my presidency, the Celtic Tiger was well and truly running around the country. In my time we were able to bring the new sponsorship model on board and the reason we were able to do so was realising how well the economy was doing, and the capability of businesses to take the model on board. There were concerns—I won't call it criticism—that the model we were bringing on board was going to disenfranchise counties, but the opposite turned out to be the case. In fairness, counties had worries, but it worked out very well for them.

"There was also the media deal we did in my time. There won't be one of those done again. That's nothing to do with me—one of my specialties from a work point of view would be negotiation and purchasing—but times are very different now."

That means the GAA must take a step back and look at what it can do to facilitate people. If the bottom line is that there aren't hungry shareholders looking to squeeze every last cent out of the business, then there's room to manoeuvre.

"Take ticket prices," says Brennan. "From an economic point of view, a few years ago that was less of an issue because commercial income was expected to become far more important than ticket income.

"Now the downturn has come and commercial income's a lot tighter. From a Croke Park point of view, it's still a strong brand."

The strength of the brand can be augmented by the odd imaginative economic measure. Take the decision to slash prices for the All-Ireland senior hurling replay from €80 to €50. Generous, says Seán Kelly—and necessary to keep people on side.

"You can do that for a replay and management usually row in because they see the logic of it—and that's the key thing. It's easy to make such decisions usually because everyone sees the logic to them. They're generous decisions to make and it's only an organisation which is basically amateur can do that.

"A professional sports organisation wouldn't be in a position to do that because they're tied into all sorts of commercial contracts, not to mind the obligation to maximise revenue utterly at all times. The GAA's been more cognisant of people's position than many people realise, with ticket packages and deals for clubs and so on. That's important because if it didn't act then people would get browned off. If they felt the GAA was really trying to milk things they'd be inclined to walk away.

"If the GAA didn't show it was aware of what was happening in the wider economy, you'd find people just wouldn't attend games or help out in their clubs."

——

It's interesting that Kelly says people aren't that aware of the GAA's ticket packaging. It's of a piece with the occasional perception of the Association as conservative or old-fashioned, though Dessie Farrell rebuts this elegantly in another part of this book. And, in fairness, it's a perception the GAA works hard to change.

"One exercise we undertook," says Nickey Brennan, "something that didn't have huge significance attached to it at the time, was the rebranding of the Association, something that people in marketing would acknowledge as hugely significant. Before that the perception was that the GAA had a lot of history but was stale in terms of image. We revitalised that by bringing in the Brand Union to look at the situation, and they made a presentation on that to the Central Council.

"Now, many people would see Central Council as a conservative group, and some people were concerned about how they'd view this development. I was gobsmacked at the end of the presentation by how much Central Council was taking on board; they might have been die-hard GAA people, but they accepted what we were trying to do. That was important and that's the reason why, while we're in tougher economic times, the GAA is still a very important brand, and one that businesses want to be associated with. You cannot expect deals to be as lucrative as they were five to six years ago. Nevertheless those deals are still very good. Yes, the number on the cheque won't be as high, but it won't be that far away from what it was."

Intriguingly, Brennan echoes the director-general when it comes to looking around for the best deal in broadcasting and media partnerships.

"The other challenge is that media outlets generally in Ireland are struggling, which is one constraint. The GAA is going to be faced with a big decision in terms of bringing in another media organisation— maybe not in the next round of negotiations, but probably the time after that. Who are we talking about here? We're talking about Sky.

"I agree with Páraic Duffy's views on that, but nobody could turn around and say 'forget that, it's never going to happen'. Why? It would be irresponsible from an economic point of view, for one thing. They're people who can bring our games to other parts of the world, possibly better than Setanta can, but there are other outlets who are looking for new sources of material for themselves. Then you have online, which is a whole other world. I have an Ipad that I run everything off these days, television, Sky Sports, the whole lot.

"So there are many more opportunities there now which weren't around maybe five or six years ago. I'd agree with Páraic on that, because as director-general your challenge is to deliver services— coaching, grants, whatever—and to do so you have to get a source of revenue."

The ambition out of the strategic plan is to up the 'recycling' figure to 88 per cent; it's at 80 per cent now, but it's got to be 80 per cent of something. "That's what's important—the bigger the pot, the more that'll be distributed."

True, but what about looking at the pot another way? In a worst-case scenario the GAA can always cut its cloth according to its measure, says Kelly. By cutting its cloth, of course, we mean cutting back—downsizing, as the *Kerryman* puts it.

"The great thing about an organisation like the GAA is that it can adapt to whatever circumstances are there, economic circumstances in particular. It can downsize. For instance, if things got really bad, then the GAA can say 'expenses are 50 cent a mile; we'll have to cut those to 40 or 30'. This year reducing the price of All-Ireland tickets from €80 to €50 was a master stroke—it showed that the GAA was cognisant of people's circumstances, and it explains why the GAA is, to some extent, insulated from the recession more than most. That was proven this year in particular with attendances. People are following their teams still.

"The GAA has less to fear from the recession than other organisations, though if it had more money it could do more, obviously."

The cut in ticket prices for the All-Ireland replay was indeed a master stroke, as Kelly says. What other master strokes are possible, though? The men I spoke to had no shortage of suggestions.

Chapter 37 ~

EUROPE, NOWLAN PARK AND THE NEW DEMOGRAPHY: CHALLENGES AND LEFT-FIELD ANSWERS

The odd time someone will bring it up in a murmur, like it's a secret password, which is probably the way they're thinking of it. You whisper it and shazam!—all is well with the GAA's finances.

Europe. Occasionally someone will point out that Irish games, being uniquely Irish and part of our cultural identity, well, isn't there some way we could get funding from Europe to help us buy hurleys or something. I mean, there's so much money there flowing around . . .

"That's a slack day's column for a sportswriter, really," says Seán Kelly, who has MEP attached to his name these days. "Europe has very clear guidelines regarding how money is spent. It must operate within the Treaties and sport is not something it'd fund directly. We have, after the Lisbon Treaty, an EU competence area for sport, which will operate from 2014 to 2020, but that would relate to big ticket items, joint events and so on.

"The idea that you could go to Europe for funding to help run your organisation—the GAA, the FAI, the IRFU, whoever—just wouldn't work. There are 27 countries involved. If they were all looking for money the budget wouldn't be long disappearing."

There are cultural events the GAA is involved in which could receive European funding, but it's certainly not the case that a county board, say, could get money from the EU to pay off its debts. "That notion is there, that there is funding in Europe for everything. That's a compliment to the EU, but there is a limit."

What about freedom of movement for workers, a core European principle? Is there any danger of a test case to be taken there about, say, club or county transfers within the GAA?

Again, Kelly's sceptical.

"There's a big difference between freedom of movement and freedom of transfer. There is freedom of movement for people working or in terms of recognition of their qualifications, but a sports organisation would be entitled to have their own rules to determine who'd be allowed to play with whom. That doesn't restrict movement. It restricts eligibility to play within the rules of that organisation, so I don't think that would hold up."

———

In any case, there are enough in-house issues for the GAA to address rather than worrying about potential legal issues down the line. Kelly and Nickey Brennan alike are particularly concerned with one aspect of modern inter-county management and its economic repercussions.

"As we've said, the big infrastructural projects go on the back burner in a recession," says Kelly. "Even though those would generate revenue and employment. You've got to be practical. We've probably reached our maximum in terms of the number of inter-county coaches—paid coaches—at the moment. We've got to be careful when it comes to inter-county managers—not so much in paying them, but in terms of the team that comes with them. That should be controlled more tightly, and maybe guidelines should be drawn up in terms of budgeting in that area."

Brennan goes even further and raises an interesting question. How many people not immediately recognised as GAA employees derive a significant amount of their income from the Association?

"Over the last ten to 12 years a whole industry has sprung up about the GAA," he says. "Years ago you had a physio and the players went to him. Now the physio goes to the players at the county ground or training venue, and there's another physio. And a masseur. And a stats man, and a nutritionist and a psychologist, and so on. It'd be interesting to see just how many people see the GAA as an important part of their income for the year.

"I'm not referring specifically to a physio attached to a county team either, but a physio who gets a lot of GAA referrals. It all comes back, though, to the strategic plan, which has to operate within a budget. You can do what some counties do and spend money they don't have—the obvious question is how do these people think those debts will be paid off—or you can do what some counties do, genuinely, and that is to run their affairs according to their budget."

Interestingly, Brennan echoes a GPA point about bringing more business savvy into the GAA: "Sometimes we almost have too much democracy in the GAA. Just before I came in as president we started appointing full-time secretaries, and the thinking at that time was that they'd become CEOs of those counties, the guy who'd make hard calls and keep officers in line.

"In all honesty, the suspicion at the time was that some of those appointment decisions were probably a bit parochial; I always felt it would take the second appointment, if you like, to show the type of person who'd be needed. A strong CEO with GAA in his DNA would also have hard-nosed business experience and would be able to put processes in place for the county to function properly. He'd be able to stand up to a powerful county team manager and say to him, 'You can appoint whoever to do whatever so long as you stay within your budget. If you stay within this figure we don't mind what you do if you operate within those resources.'"

Again, you can hear an echo there of another issue raised in the book—the county board spending cap. Kelly says that "makes sense", but points to one flaw in the five-year rule which moves county board officers along after that period of time.

"Everyone has to budget. Everyone has to plan and counties which wouldn't have great resources might be given a grant to meet their costs—so long as they were willing to live within their means, so to speak.

"The other point is that with the five-year rule you have much more turnover in officers, and the ethos of the steady hand—particularly the treasurer who was inclined to treat the money as if it were his own—is not as strong as it was, perhaps. There can be a temptation for officers, for chairmen, to say 'in my five years we'll win an All-Ireland, and we'll give it everything to do so'. But it's the next man in, five years down the line, who has to deal with the mess."

———

When you ask for ideas that go against the grain, both men respond quickly. Brennan advocates tearing up prejudices about the location of games; Kelly suggests involving the Department of Education in recognising teachers who volunteer to coach hurling and football.

As a former teacher the Kerry native is familiar with the schools' relationship with the GAA, and it's a cause of concern for him: "There's so much pressure now on teachers in terms of extra duties and so on. If you lose the goodwill of the teachers you won't be able to get coaches into the schools in the first place. That's a very important balancing act—encouraging teachers to be involved, to give them back-up and support rather than full-time coaches, because you may not be able to afford the latter in the long term."

Paying teachers extra for coaching is a crude solution, though.

"That's a tricky one, because where do you draw the line? If you say we'll pay the man coaching the senior team, what about the person training the first year team? You could do more harm than good. If you were to do something like that it could be in the form of a general subvention to the school for buses, gear or whatever. Giving money to an individual would break the link to the voluntary ethos as well. You might also be able to do something in terms of the Department of Education recognising what's being done as extra teaching hours, and extra pay, maybe."

For decades, of course, the GAA benefited from a vast cohort of unpaid coaches—Christian Brothers and priests, who have disappeared from the schools in large measure. "It's left a huge void," says Kelly. "A lot of schools haven't replaced them, and they've fallen off the radar as a result. Some of the slack has been taken up by clubs falling in to help, while lay teachers have also become involved. It's worked out better than you'd have imagined, but it's a challenge because once you lose a school in terms of the games, it's very hard to get it back. You have to encourage schools to keep their tradition because nothing is worse than seeing a great GAA school give up that tradition."

For his part, Nickey Brennan has a proposal which would help a county board in financial straits—if they were willing to set tradition aside.

"From my time on there were no major ground redevelopments, though there were grounds that had to be upgraded on a small scale— you're talking about a million here and a million there, not huge projects. In my view the GAA made the mistake some years earlier of spending a lot of money on grounds with no strategic direction on that spending. We need to be imaginative here.

"Take Walsh Park in Waterford. I've floated this idea—why spend money redeveloping that venue when Waterford could pop 30 minutes up the road to Nowlan Park to play home games in the Munster championship? So what if it's in another province? It's win-win because right now Waterford can't play a home game in the Munster championship and therefore they're deprived of the gate. Give Kilkenny five per cent of the gate and take the rest.

"Okay, I'm wearing a Kilkenny hat, but if I were the Waterford treasurer and playing a game in Kilkenny brought in €70,000 or €80,000 in revenue, I'd say why not? What's the big deal when the alternative is nothing? When Croke Park was being redeveloped Kilkenny and other Leinster counties went to play in Thurles, another province. What about it?"

———

Looking ahead, Kelly warns that the economic situation has the potential to shrink the pool of potential championship winners and leave other counties further and further behind.

"Counties have to be careful, because you can put too much money into trying to be successful. The GAA can't be carrying debts for what are current activities; if it did, it'd go under pretty quickly. You can see how counties try to raise funds—golf classics, supporters' clubs, you name it—but there has to be a limit. You can't buy success, and you can't just pay everyone what they want to get success.

"There's a danger that only a few counties will be able to afford inter-county success, and the others will fall further behind. That's something the GAA must be wary of, because as we're not an international organisation, we have to be sure the GAA is strong all over the country. Success is a very important element in keeping it strong, and if counties who were in contention start to fall off, that'll damage the GAA.

"Take Offaly, very good through the sixties to the nineties, but they've fallen off the pace now and they'll find it hard to be competitive again. Coming back to the point about having soccer and rugby games in Croke Park again, if that were to happen then there might be an argument for taking any extra revenue raised there and instead of spreading it all over the country, it could be focused on counties which have a tradition, which are willing to put in the effort, and which need the resources. If those counties were backed for five to six years you could see how they went, and it might be better to be strategic in that way than democratic, if you like, and give everyone a shake."

When it comes to everyone getting a shake, the Kerryman confesses a particular annoyance on one economic question. The vast spending power wielded by the hundreds of thousands of people who swamp Dublin for the All-Ireland series is worthy of recognition, he feels.

"I often think the GAA doesn't get enough credit for the revenue it generates in the broader economy, particularly with big games in Dublin, for instance. I never got the impression that custom was appreciated by the business community there—matches, concerts and so on. I think it was recognised to a certain degree when rugby and soccer were played in Croke Park because businesses in Dublin realised they'd have lost those games and all that business to England otherwise. But All-Ireland finals and semi-finals, all that activity, sometimes that isn't appreciated compared to other towns around the country.

"Someone like Jimmy O'Brien in Killarney would tell you that the best day of the year for his business would be Cork and Kerry in Fitzgerald Stadium; they'd be grateful for that, while I never got that sense of appreciation from businesses in Dublin. It'd be nice to see that. I suppose they know those games are going to happen; they know they'll get the business. Maybe that's why there's no great sense that they should put something back in."

Invited to peer into the crystal ball, Nickey Brennan doesn't see the open draw hurtling towards us the way others do. For him the future in terms of championship structure, for instance, may be pretty familiar to us from the past.

"Given the nature of a knock-out championship you can't be sure who'll play whom, but let's look at it in the two sports. In hurling it's as close as you can get it, probably, with a Munster and a Leinster championship. Those two competitions are both delivering a decent number of games, and I'd say the prospect of an open draw— completely open—is nil. I'd say there are no prospects of that for the foreseeable future, and there is an open draw of sorts already when you're knocked out of your province.

"We need to remember, too, that there's no need for the structure of one to follow the other when it comes to the football and hurling championships. If you took four groups of eight in football, you're going to have a much more formalised structure, that's true. But you're going to lose the one ingredient that's inherent in the GAA more so than any other sport, maybe—local and provincial rivalry.

"You're losing an awful lot with that. If Carlow play Donegal, for instance, then that's of no interest to a lot of people. If Carlow play Wicklow in Aughrim there's a good buzz in both counties about that, and all of that is without getting into the chances of people from Carlow, for instance, driving up from Carlow to Ballybofey or Letterkenny for a game like that. Local rivalries embody what we're about. And when you come to football, there are only about ten counties—being generous—with a shot at the All-Ireland. Most will be also-rans, so the current set-up at least gives counties a chance to make a burst every now and again."

And when that burst comes with a specific target in mind, it's not a matter of making it out of an artificial grouping system.

"I'd have often asked officials in less successful counties about that—how they keep going when they know, deep down, at the start of every year they've little chance of success. They always said that the attitude had to be that this particular year was the one they might make a provincial final, say, the Clare hurlers or the Leitrim footballers. The provincial championships attract a lot of negativity but you have to look back at some of those great days. They're what can sustain a county, and you wouldn't have them if, say, Carlow beat Donegal in a Group A game or whatever. It wouldn't be the same as winning a Leinster semi-final, say, in a million years."

———

Another deep thinker on GAA issues is even more radical. Eamon O'Shea sees amalgamation at county level a recipe for hurling success, for instance.

"The next layer of counties—Westmeath, Antrim, Laois etc.— could model themselves on the Dublin model in terms of expenditure. There are economies of scale involved that could be used. Laois and Westmeath, for instance, could be combined to improve standards: you could have joint championships.

"Now the obvious reaction from the county boards involved would be, 'God, you couldn't do that'; you must start identifying elite players and give them something to aim for, something to drive them on. But again, you can't have *ad hoc* plans on that dreamed up by people who move on within a couple of years. You have to have structure."

Not that structure is sacred. Take O'Shea's clear-eyed views on the Munster hurling championship—delivered, in fairness, a few months before he became Tipperary senior hurling manager.

"There are four distinct seasons now: the pre-season with the Waterford Crystal or equivalent competition, the league, the provincial championship and then the All-Ireland. If you are managing a team these are four distinct seasons. In the first you're looking at getting rid of people. In the second you're looking at how the team is developing and progressing. In the third season you have a championship, fair enough, but you have half an eye even then on the fourth championship, because it's not winner-takes-all in the third season, and you can experiment a little. It changes, then. You get to an All-Ireland quarter-final and you know there's a difference to the Munster championship, say. But sacred cows are under threat from economic circumstances."

O'Shea's day job with NUIG means he pays a lot of attention to changes in demographics; he wonders if the GAA should do the same.

"The changing economic circumstances mean in rural areas, in particular, numbers will necessitate change. And the other side of that is some of the huge superclubs in Dublin, for instance, could be broken up.

"But the democratic nature of the GAA means it's hard to do those things by diktat—it'd be hard to announce 'well, there are only five viable clubs in this part of rural Galway' or 'there are only eight senior clubs in this part of Tipperary'. What people would focus on there, of course, would be the identities of the clubs involved rather than the substantive issue of standards.

"I'm not sure the scale of the rural problem generally has filtered through to the decision-makers, let alone the GAA—how rural life is impacted by demographic change, by economic decline, by emigration. As it hasn't filtered through at official level, I doubt it has been recognised at GAA level, though a GAA club would know well the impact of two or three young lads going to Australia for a year—not even emigrating—because the club would know 'without them we'll only be able to tog out without competing'."

The quandary is, as O'Shea sees it, a rural model which is now more successful in urban areas than in the countryside where it first took hold: "It's odd that while the GAA was founded as a rural organisation, great work is being done in the cities, and there is a danger that the rurality may be left behind. I think it just has to be reconfigured, and in that context the economics of the club game is something that people don't pay enough attention to—say, the timing of fixtures, how they're attached to the inter-county team and its success, optimal venues.

"In Tipp attendances were down at club games in 2011, for instance, and that may have been down in part to fatigue—the county team had been in three All-Ireland finals and 2011 wasn't as successful as 2010. But it might also have related to the fact that a lot of the games weren't competitive enough—or local enough. If I were back home I might go to a game in McDonagh Park (Nenagh) between local rivals whereas I mightn't head up to Semple Stadium for a game between a team from the South and one from the North. One of those local rivals in Nenagh might be more likely to win, but you never know, while for me the game in Semple Stadium just wouldn't be local enough."

The Tipperary man is also one of the few GAA people to speak frankly about the Association's challenges with other sports.

"I think we've been too mealy-mouthed about the competition from rugby, soccer and other sports. I think we need to confront this straight up. I see down the Prom here in Galway the Connacht Rugby flags, here in Salthill. Yet can I name the Connacht squad? No, yet I'm interested in sport, and rugby in particular.

"Let's compete here. We're in competition. I have a ten-year old and if he says to me he wants to go off playing rugby—well, to me it's up to us in the GAA to make our sports very attractive, and to make his heroes very attractive to him. And of course, he wouldn't recognise a Galway hurler because our hurlers aren't marketed properly—they are marketed to an extent, but they're not marketed very well. It's a two-tier thing. You can't stop kids from playing whatever they want, but you can make the GAA more attractive to them. We need to put more resources into marketing, coaching, and into fighting the battle.

"Now you can do that in a pleasant way. I have no problem with Pearse Stadium being used for rugby, for instance, because economically it would only make sense for somewhere the size of Galway to have Pearse Stadium hosting the city's soccer team on a Friday, the rugby team on a Saturday and the hurling or football team on Sunday—with a single ticket available for the three events, by the way. You've got to market it more attractively.

"Here in Galway you can't market hurling based on the historical accident that 30 years ago the county won two All-Irelands in hurling, in 1987 and 1988. You couldn't market hurling to kids based on that, because they can't remember yesterday."

Mind you, marketing involves players as well.

"There's no onus on players to make themselves available to market the games, obviously, but there's another way to look at that," he says. "If I were an inter-county manager (which O'Shea had become by the date of publication) I'd have no problem with players talking to the media with some provisos—that they recognise that what they say is going to be published, for instance—but I certainly would have no issue with a player interview appearing in the week of a big game. A lot of managers would have a problem with that, but I couldn't give a damn. To me it has no relevance at all, unless you have a teenager starting out. A 23, 24-year old should have his performance impacted more by what I say to him on the Friday night before a game than by what he told a journalist the Thursday week beforehand.

"But there is an issue of marketability. To me even the hurler is different to the footballer—hurlers can be more modest and self-effacing than footballers, and you can often see they're less comfortable in interviews. Certainly, though, I think we need to do more to help players communicate in order to, not cash in, but to help create a dividend for everybody: the game wins; players win."

Chapter 38 ∽

CONCLUSION: VALUE FOR MONEY?

The tension mentioned in the introduction is something Seán Kelly returns to again and again, but only to show that in that particular struggle—economic imperatives and amateur ethos—one side tends to have the upper hand.

"History shows that that tension is managed pretty well. We still have the amateur ethos that everyone grew up with, with people giving their time—particularly at local level—voluntarily. People make do. I'd say the number of people who'd be disgruntled is low, that they're few and far between, and you'd always have some people who'll be unhappy in an organisation the size of the GAA. The fact that it continues to thrive and hold its own, particularly at grass-roots level, shows to me that the number of people who walk away is low. And perhaps those who walk away come back eventually. Some of them, anyway."

Like Catholicism? You can lapse but you can never really leave?

"That's a good way of putting it. People would ask me do I miss the GAA. I miss being involved, but I keep in touch. I meet people still, I read the reports in the paper, I go to matches. A lot depends on the level of involvement you want. I suppose people find their own level. You'll have people who find they're too involved, but that they're like that all their life."

One of his successors makes the same point: "We get involved because it's an interest, it's what you were reared with and you want to hand it on," says Christy Cooney. "I don't discount what people 'outside' the GAA think of the Association. I find that people rate us enormously highly—higher than we rate ourselves. The standing the Assocation has from other sports, from the general community, for what it brings to Irish society . . . It didn't surprise me, but it was a lot more than I thought. It just showed me the strength of the brand."

Still, there's economics in the title of the book. The last word should go to the experts in the field, and Eamon O'Shea belies the general reputation of economists by being upbeat.

"Some of the economic issues that are out there may not affect the GAA," he says. "At the moment, for instance, there may be a lot of rugby clubs in Europe looking at the Heineken Cup and losing a bit of interest because Irish teams have won it in 2006, 2008, 2009, 2011 and 2012. The ERC are probably thinking of TV audiences if that continues. So that may become a commercial pressure, but there may also be an issue in European law along the lines of unfair State aid because of the 40 per cent tax rebate for playing in Ireland, so there could be repercussions for the Irish teams there as well.

"In large measure the GAA is safe from that because European employment law wouldn't apply to cultural activities."

His colleague in economics, John Considine, says that the recession has concentrated in the GAA as much as elsewhere.

"Looking to the medium or long term the recession has affected several areas. Pay for play is out of the picture, for instance, because of that, and issues like emigration and people fitting sport around work are also concerns. One slight worry would be a tendency to boom and bust, particularly in clubs—the regime which spends and leaves it to the next regime to carry the can, as others have said. GAA clubs should get back to core values—I'm not saying 'jumpers for goalposts'; you need a certain level—but you need to concentrate on activities on the field. That's your core activity."

O'Shea addresses the bottom line question about the GAA for an economist. Does it offer value for money?

"I had a few students from America some years ago and I got them to ask people what they were willing to pay for their GAA club memberships and what they were actually paying. Relative to what people were paying for tennis club memberships, or soccer or rugby clubs, people were getting huge value. Family membership, for four people, €75. If you go down to the new gym here in the college I'm paying €600 for membership for a family of five—and that's with a reduction.

"What do you get in a GAA club? Coaching for the youngsters a couple of nights a week, a game at the weekend, all without even getting into the intangibles—a sense of belonging to the community, attachment to place, the kids linking to schools, the sharing of knowledge and information.

"It's also egalitarian and democratic. You may want to join a different kind of club because you've decided you want to meet a different kind of person, but if you're talking about solidarity and some sense of egalitarian values, which I believe in, then here you have a construct which suits that—whether you are from social housing or a big house up on the hill and earning lots of money. Given our tendency to privatise ourselves—in education, in healthcare, in our cars, even—the GAA field is one of the last public spaces around. It's one of the places where you can be exposed to the variety of the human condition. There is very little in Irish life which is better value for money than membership of a GAA club."

INDEX